Your
Horoscope
2023

....

Cancer

22 June – 22 July

igloobooks

igloobooks

Published in 2022
First published in the UK by Igloo Books Ltd
An imprint of Igloo Books Ltd
Cottage Farm, NN6 0BJ, UK
Owned by Bonnier Books
Sveavägen 56, Stockholm, Sweden
www.igloobooks.com

0722 001
2 4 6 8 10 9 7 5 3 1
ISBN 978-1-80108-399-7

Written by Sally Kirkman
Additional content by Belinda Campbell and Denise Evans

Designed by Richard Sykes
Edited by Katie Taylor

Printed and manufactured in China

CONTENTS
· · · · · · · · · · · · · · · · · ·

INTRODUCTION
. . . .

This 15-month guide has been designed and written to give a concise and accessible insight into both the nature of your star sign and the year ahead. Divided into two main sections, the first section of this guide will give you an overview of your character in order to help you understand how you think, perceive the world and interact with others and – perhaps just as importantly – why. You'll soon see that your zodiac sign is not just affected by a few stars in the sky, but by planets, elements, and a whole host of other factors, too.

The second section of this guide is made up of daily forecasts. Use these to increase your awareness of what might appear on your horizon so that you're better equipped to deal with the days ahead. While this should never be used to dictate your life, it can be useful to see how your energies might be affected or influenced, which in turn can help you prepare for what life might throw your way.

By the end of these 15 months, these two sections should have given you a deeper understanding and awareness of yourself and, in turn, the world around you. There are never any definite certainties, but with an open mind you will find guidance for what might be, and learn to take more control of your own destiny.

THE CHARACTER
OF THE CRAB

. . . .

Cancer is the cardinal sign that kicks off summer in the zodiac calendar, and is also the first of the water signs. These summery Crabs love rounding up family and friends for a day at the beach. Creativity surrounds them, whether that means whipping up a meal for loved ones or redecorating the home. Cancerians saturate themselves with the latest trends in food, fashion, art and culture. They will have had that trendy new artist's work hanging on their walls long before anyone else can jump on the bandwagon. Or perhaps the masterpiece that Cancerians love most is their own, such as with artistic Crab Frida Kahlo. Their creative juices flow constantly and freely, and are born from a deep love and empathy.

For Cancerians, home is always where the heart is. Born in the fourth house signifying the home and family, they are best known for their unfailing love and caring nature. Some of the most beloved figures in history, such as Nelson Mandela and Diana, Princess of Wales, have been nurturing Cancerians. These homebody Crabs will usually make more of an effort than most to visit their family, wanting to surround themselves in loving and supportive atmospheres. Cancerians also love to invite people into their own home, hosting dinners, movie nights and plenty of parties – especially in their younger years. Friends and family should be careful of the crabby side, however. 'It's my party and I'll cry if I want to' probably rings true for most Cancerians. They can be overly sensitive, and are renowned for their almighty moods. Security is what they crave, and the need to settle their sometimes-unpredictable emotions.

THE CRAB

Tough on the outside yet vulnerable on the inside, the Crab symbolises many of the key traits associated with Cancerians. Those born under this sign have a negative polarity, which can mean that they are prone to processing thoughts and feelings internally, and may retreat into the safety of their own shells for long periods of time. Whilst their exterior may appear hard, Cancerians reveal their soft sensitivity to those who wait. A cosy and secure home life is an essential part of their happiness. Whether they prefer to live alone like the hermit crab or as part of a large family, Cancerians often need to spend quality time on their own for some peaceful self-reflection. With the love and support of family and friends, they can be coaxed from whatever sandy bay they may have decided to disappear into temporarily. The Crab is a unique balance of strength and vulnerability, which makes Cancerians treasured family members and fiercely reliable friends or partners.

THE MOON

The mother of the sky and the guardian sign of the zodiac calendar, the Moon and Cancerians are bonded by emotion. The Moon is the closest astronomical body to Earth, which is maybe why it feels so familiar, and why it governs homebody Cancer. There is a reassurance in being able to look up at the sky and watch the Moon's cyclical patterns, a constant quality that Cancerians are likely to find comfort in. The Moon's gravitational pull dictates Earth's tides, so any water signs will feel the influence of the Moon greatly. For Cancerians, their emotional ties to home and family are where the maternal influence of the Moon comes into effect. Cancerians are best known for their caring side, but this can turn into a worrisome nature or a tendency to smother those closest to them if they become ruled by their emotions. Both male and female Cancerians have an emotional intuition that is unparalleled, thanks to the Moon's guidance.

ELEMENTS, MODES AND POLARITIES

Each sign is made up of a unique combination of three defining groups: elements, modes and polarities. Each of these defining parts can manifest themselves in good and bad ways and none should be seen as a positive or a negative – including the polarities! Just like a jigsaw puzzle, piecing these groups together can help illuminate why each sign has certain characteristics and help us find a balance.

ELEMENTS

Fire: Dynamic and adventurous, signs with fire in them can be extroverted. Others are naturally drawn to them because of the positive light they give off, as well as their high levels of energy and confidence.

Earth: Signs with the earth element are steady and driven with their ambitions. They make for a solid friend, parent or partner due to their grounded influence and nurturing nature.

Air: The invisible element that influences each of the other elements significantly, air signs will provide much-needed perspective to others with their fair thinking, verbal skills and key ideas.

Water: Warm in the shallows and freezing as ice. This mysterious element is essential to the growth of everything around it, through its emotional depth and empathy.

MODES

Cardinal: Pioneers of the calendar, cardinal signs jump-start each season and are the energetic go-getters.

Fixed: Marking the middle of the calendar, fixed signs represent and value steadiness and reliability.

Mutable: As the seasons end, the mutable signs adapt and give themselves over gladly to the promise of change.

POLARITIES

Positive: Typically extroverted, positive signs take physical action and embrace outside stimulus in their life.

Negative: Usually introverted, negative signs value emotional development and experiencing life from the inside out.

CANCER IN BRIEF

The table below shows the key attributes of Cancerians. Use it for quick reference and to understand more about this fascinating sign.

SYMBOL	RULING PLANET	MODE	ELEMENT	HOUSE
The Crab	Moon	Cardinal	Water	Fourth

COLOUR	BODY PART	POLARITY	GENDER	POLAR SIGN
White/Silver	Breasts	Negative	Feminine	Capricorn

ROMANTIC RELATIONSHIPS

. . . .

Born in the fourth house of family and home, security can be essential to Cancerians in a relationship. Not ones for living a life made up of one-night stands, even though they might try it out in their younger years, they want to find a stable and long-term relationship. Family can be hugely important to Cancerians, so they will more often than not be asking whether they see themselves having children with potential partners on the first or second date. Whilst security is crucial, this isn't always the right approach for finding love. Allowing themselves to be vulnerable to others is an important practice for any hard-shelled Cancerians struggling to let love in.

Love is usually felt deeply and intensely by Cancerians. Being so in tune and receptive to both their own and their partner's emotions makes them some of the most intuitive lovers in the entire zodiac calendar. Cancerians often instinctively know what others need, without them having to express it. Such is their sensitivity, Cancerians will be mindful of always pleasing their lovers. This innate ability to pick up on what others want makes them hugely desirable.

Cancerians may be able to tap into emotions to form meaningful relationships, but this also has its disadvantages. They can be prone to emotional outbursts as damaging as a burst dam, or as irritating as a leaky tap. Whilst Cancerians might need to develop emotional control, an empathetic spouse who won't take their partner's outbursts to heart will help bring balance. A steady earth sign can complement water perfectly, forming a nurturing and mutually beneficial bond.

The cardinal aspect of Cancerians will usually make them happy to make the first move in love. They will also be likely to admire a fellow cardinal partner that matches their go-getter attitude.

ARIES: COMPATIBILITY 1/5

This pair shares opposite characteristics that don't always attract, sadly. A homely creature, the Cancerian may find the Arian's adventurous roaming too uncomfortable and unsettling. Conversely, the Arian will not thrive in this relationship if constricted or held back in any way by the Cancerian. However, these water and fire signs are true opposites, and therefore can stand to learn a great deal from one another. In particular, the Cancerian can teach the Arian to be more considered before acting, whilst the Arian can teach the Cancerian to be less worrisome.

TAURUS: COMPATIBILITY 5/5

Placed two positions apart on the zodiac calendar, a Cancerian and Taurean share a bond that can feel just like home. The Cancerian's frequent displays of love are deep and clear, like two names carved into a tree! The intensity of the Taurean's affection, mixed with the Cancerian's head-over-heels approach, can see these two lovers running to the altar and settling down with babies – not always in that order. Here are two signs that will do anything for each other, and will usually prefer their own little party of two.

GEMINI: COMPATIBILITY 2/5

This air and water pairing can feel too far apart personality-wise to make a good match, but the differences could actually prove to be strengthening. The Geminian is led by the mind and the Cancerian by emotion. These contrasting perspectives can lead to misunderstandings and arguments if the line of communication isn't clear. The Geminian can help the Cancerian communicate thoughts and feelings aloud rather than keeping them bottled up, while the Cancerian can provide lessons on the value of sensitivity. With so much to learn from one another, understanding and acceptance is vital to their success.

CANCER: COMPATIBILITY 4/5

The love that two Cancerians have can run as deep and mysterious as the seas from which water signs spring. The priority of creating a strong family home will be a shared goal for these two lovers, and building a large family unit will likely bring joy and satisfaction to them both. Co-parenting is something that this nurturing pair will likely excel at. With the right amount of personal space afforded to one another, these two will be able to keep their heads above water and enjoy exploring each other's depths.

LEO: COMPATIBILITY 3/5

Leo is ruled by the Sun and Cancer by the Moon, so this pairing can feel as different as night and day. However, the Lion and the Crab can also find that they have plenty in common to form a lasting love. Born in the fourth and fifth houses that partly signify family and children, the Leonian and Cancerian share a fundamental desire to find that long-term partner to settle down with. Security is essential for the Cancerian and the fixed side of the steadfast Leonian can provide just that. This power couple could go the distance if their differences are embraced.

VIRGO: COMPATIBILITY 3/5

A practical-minded Virgoan could be the balancing force that a Cancerian needs in a partner. The Virgoan will feel loved and protected by the nurturing Cancerian, but by contrast the Cancerian can at times feel hurt by the naturally critical Virgoan. Thanks to ruling planet Mercury, the Virgoan's strong communication skills should help them patch up any problems. The earth element in Virgo and the cardinal influence in Cancer can make for a driven couple, so any loving ambitions that these two share will likely be realised together.

LIBRA: COMPATIBILITY 3/5

Ruled by the planet of love and the emotions of the Moon, the romance between a Libran and Cancerian can read like an epic poem. The Libran's love for aesthetics will be particularly attractive to the creative Crab, and encourage many artistic endeavours. The home that these two could build together might well be a thing of beauty and harmony. Both cardinal characters, the Libran and Cancerian match each other's energetic attitudes, but may fight for power in the relationship. Whilst their introvert and extrovert tendencies could clash, the Libran's search for peace could help make this relationship last.

SCORPIO: COMPATIBILITY 2/5

These two water signs could easily drown in a pool of emotion. Ruled by Mars, the Scorpian's passion for the Cancerian will be intense, and the Cancerian's feelings are highly likely to be mutual. Claws and stingers at the ready, explosive disagreements could see both sides getting hurt. Both can be stubborn and unwilling to bend in an argument, which may result in them parting ways quickly. However, once these two decide that they want to be together, they can experience a love that is unfailing in its loyalty.

· · · · · · · · · · · · · · · · ·

SAGITTARIUS: COMPATIBILITY 1/5

A Cancerian might end up feeling lost with an adventuring
wanderer that is a Sagittarian. The Sagittarian can help bring
out a worldlier side to the Cancerian and show that a sense of
community can stretch larger than the end of the road. With the
Crab, the roaming Sagittarian can learn the benefits of settling
down in a loving relationship. These two have contrasting
masculine and feminine energies that can complement each
other greatly, if their differences are nurtured rather than
discouraged. Plenty of personal time needs to be allowed to
reap the many rewards from when opposites attract.

CAPRICORN: COMPATIBILITY 5/5

Opposites on the zodiac calendar, a Capricornian and Cancerian
can experience a tenacious love. Symbolised often with a fish's
tail, the Sea Goat that represents the Capricornian can swim
happily in the Cancerian's warm waters. The Cancerian can
indeed help coax a playfulness from the Capricornian that others
don't always see. The Capricornian is ruled by the authoritative
planet of Saturn, so could be a strong parenting partner for the
family orientated Cancerian. If these two hard workers fall in
love with one another, the dedication that they share could
be staggering.

AQUARIUS: COMPATIBILITY 1/5

A rebellious Aquarian and security-seeking Cancerian are not always an obvious match romantically. Whilst their core character differences may be the cause of arguments, if these two can find common interests that can cement a foundation for friendship then love could still bloom. If the Cancerian can help the intellectual Aquarian to engage emotionally, then both could mutually benefit from this unlikely but special meeting of the heart and mind. Common ground to share and foreign lands to explore will be what's needed for the Aquarian and Cancerian to find a lasting love together.

PISCES: COMPATIBILITY 4/5

These two feminine and water signs can be a vision of romance together. The Cancerian recognises the changeable river of emotion that runs within Pisces, and identifies with the alternating speeds, directions and temperatures. Here are two signs that enjoy nurturing loved ones, and so their love will be built on a mutual support system. However, the Crab and Fish need to be mindful not to get swept away by the floods of emotion they are both capable of unleashing in romantic relationships. If this is kept in check, then love and compassion can flow freely.

FAMILY AND FRIENDS

. . . .

Cancerian homes are often as warm and as comforting as a cup of tea. Born into the fourth house that represents home and family, home life is of utmost importance to these expert nest-makers. Cancerians will want to make their homes an inviting environment that all the family will feel comfortable and welcome in. Capricornians make for appreciative house guests, and will be sure to notice the new artwork hanging in the artistic hallway. Cancerians who have used their creativity to decorate their own home will find that it is not wasted on aesthetic-loving Taureans, who will be full of compliments. Both Cancerians and Taureans are very much homebodies, preferring to stay in and watch a film rather than party every night, so can make highly compatible housemates.

Earth and water signs are considered to have a feminine energy and the deities associated most with the Moon are also female, so the relationships that Cancerians have with their mothers, sisters and female friends will likely help shape them greatly. The relationship with our parents plays a vital role in our overall happiness. For Cancerians, who are known for valuing family connections over most other things, this is especially applicable. Ask them to name a best friend, and they are most likely to name a parent. Cancerians likely want their own children at some stage and, if they are lucky enough to have them, will apply themselves wholeheartedly to parenting.

Cancerians are extremely intuitive beings, making them sensitive to the feelings of others. Friends and family of Cancerians might use them readily as a reliable shoulder to cry on. Cancerians are wonderful at giving loved ones reassurance and sensitive guidance, but they also expect these things in return. They can tend to dwell on the bad things that happen to them, and can hanker after constant reassurance when feeling low. When Cancerians feel like they are not receiving the sensitivity and comfort that they provide for others, they can become defensive. Retreating inwards or reacting in an overly emotional manner are both typical of Cancerians who feel like they are being attacked. Their almighty moods and grudge-holding abilities can be exhausting and alienating. Peacekeeping Libran friends could help Cancerians to balance out their emotional outbursts, whilst friendly mutable Pisceans will be able to see past the mood swings. Friends, family and Cancerians themselves will do well not to dwell too readily on disagreements and practise forgiving and forgetting. The caring gestures that Cancerians are so good at showing should hopefully remedy arguments in the long run.

MONEY AND CAREERS

· · · · · · · · · · · · · · · · · ·

Being a particular star sign will not dictate certain types of career, but it can help identify potential areas for thriving in. Conversely, to succeed in the workplace, it is just as important to understand strengths and weaknesses to achieve career and financial goals.

For the Crab sign of the zodiac calendar, working in a social sector that helps to protect the vulnerable in society might be a natural calling. Whether it's working as police officers, firefighters or nurses, or other service roles, caring Cancerians thrive in a workplace where their protective instincts can be put to good use. Whether it is full-time work or a part-time passion, giving time to help others voluntarily can be an important part of their working life. Following in the footsteps of Cancerian philanthropist Diana, Princess of Wales, who was known for her kindness and charity, may be something that Cancerians wish to work towards.

Born in the fourth house that represents a love of home mixed with a cardinal persistence, the writing profession is well suited to Cancerians. They possess the innate ability to understand emotion, and also translate it for others. Broody Cancerians should be careful of hiding away in their writing cave for too long though, as they are known for working themselves too hard. The cardinal aspect of Cancer gives this sign the driving force to leave a lasting and positive influence on the world. Seeing their words published could be a lifelong ambition for Cancerians and they may find great success, like fellow Crab Ernest Hemingway.

As with family, colleagues cannot be chosen. Therefore, it can be advantageous to use star signs to learn about their key characteristics and discover the best ways of working together. Creative and wonderfully empathetic, two Cancerians could find sharing their artistic talents an exciting collaboration. Whilst arguments could flare up, their ability to understand one another can get them back on track to working towards a shared goal.

Sea sponges for emotions, Cancerians soak up the emotions of positive and negative people in their lives, so working with the former can be essential. Optimistic Sagittarians could be just the positive colleagues to inspire less-secure Cancerians. A lack of confidence can hold this sign back professionally, so a 'fake it until you make it' attitude could do wonders for climbing the career ladder. Deep down, Cancerians are more than capable of rising to the top.

The organisational skills of the Crab are well known, and this attribute means that Cancerians are likely to succeed in their chosen career, regardless of whether they are working for someone else or managing their own business.

The satisfaction of a job well done is all this sign needs to be motivated. Money itself is generally less of a motivating factor – as long as their essential needs are provided for, Cancerians are happy to sit back slightly and spend more time with the people they love, rather than clocking up the hours in the office chasing that elusive promotion or bonus. This is certainly not to say that Cancerians lack ambition or drive, simply that they can be quite happy placing their focus on the home, once their work is sorted.

HEALTH AND WELLBEING

. . . .

Feeling things deeply, as Moon-ruled Cancerians do, means sometimes suffering from emotional insecurities and questions of self-doubt. If Cancerians find themselves sinking into anxiety, it may be that they are surrounded by too much negativity. They can be sponges for both positive and negative influences, so should review any problem areas and think how best to make improvements. A change of perspective may actually be what is required. For example, instead of wondering if they earn enough money, Cancerians should question how they can get a promotion at work. Trying to live life more fearlessly could help reduce some angst.

Spending time near water is the obvious way for Cancerians to unwind. Holidays by the coast, either home or abroad, help them to recharge their batteries and gain clarity on life. If running off to the sea isn't always feasible, taking a moment to go for a walk by a canal or pond can help them reflect on any concerns. Even a bubble bath can feel as restorative as a day at the spa.

Wellbeing practices need to be a particular priority for Cancerians. Wonderful at caring for others, they often neglect themselves. Physical exercise has been known to improve mental health and help reduce depression, and sports that lead Crabs to water, such as swimming or surfing, offer the dual benefits of both physical and emotional fitness. When exercise isn't possible, something as simple as watching a funny film could instead help lift their low moods.

Having a positive influence on the world should in turn have a positive influence on philanthropic Cancerians. Volunteering for a charity, or even setting one up, could be the legacy that they take the most joy in. They should be careful of shouldering the world's problems, however, to protect their own wellbeing. In order to truly help others, Cancerians should find and regularly practise ways of releasing worries before feeling overwhelmed. Having a place of peace and serenity in the home could help them let go of whatever stresses lie outside the front door. Weekly cleaning or decluttering sessions can also help Crabs feel more at ease.

Cancer

....

DAILY FORECASTS
for 2022

OCTOBER

. . . .

Saturday 1st

The best thing you can do today is to lie low and let everyone else get on with it. If you attempt to do anything bold or make peace, you will fail. The energy suggests that you could be exhausted if you try. Do your own thing and make the most of your weekend.

Sunday 2nd

Don't believe everything you hear today. Mercury turns direct and can cause more confusion with communication. You might think that you're out of the woods, but you're not. Partner time may soothe your soul, but you could also project your unwanted baggage onto someone unsuspecting and cause more problems.

Monday 3rd

Today you might think about romance and friendships. There could be a way to combine both and bring out your creative side too. It's possible that a new romance blossoms out of your social groups. This can give you some pleasant surprises and change the dynamics which have been suffering recently.

Tuesday 4th

Thoughts and emotions can keep you awake. You may be struggling with a change regarding relationships. It could be that you are going through a filtering process and seeing what remains when what you don't want has been discarded. Conversations can be uniquely balanced which may seem like a novelty.

Wednesday 5th

Innovative connections can bring some much-needed lightness to your soul. If you exercise strong boundaries you might find a new passion or relationship which is on a completely new level. You may need to get used to this and learn to connect from your mind and not just your emotions.

Thursday 6th

Today can be very dreamy and you might feel as if you've been whisked away to a fantasy island. Spiritual growth is occurring and it may feel fresh and new. Allow yourself to drift and imagine. Your mind and emotions can meet in the middle.

Friday 7th

Whilst floating on your cloud you may hear your inner voice telling you that what you thought was your mission has been aborted. Navigate towards what your inner compass is telling you now. This may be addictive, and you should try to keep at least one foot on the ground.

Saturday 8th

You might have a lot to think about today. Your inner compass is available, and you should check in. Retain an open heart today and allow new thoughts and feelings to flow. This afternoon you may begin to see the journey ahead and plan accordingly. Just don't weigh yourself down again.

Sunday 9th

Pluto turns direct and has finished rearranging relationships. It's up to you to deal with the fallout. A full moon is an excellent time to look back at how far you've come since spring. Pare away anything that might be impeding further progress or slowing you down.

Monday 10th

Your energy is high today and you can be extra productive. Gather more facts and do some last-minute research on a project which you're about to be heavily involved in. You could be grieving for something you've let go of recently. It's okay to honour what it once meant to you.

Tuesday 11th

Your family life could become filled with chatter now. There may be negotiations to be made or family conferences regarding fairness and equality. Legal issues are possible, and you may need to hire a professional. You could also be studying something which brings balance to your home and work lives.

Wednesday 12th

Be mindful of how you communicate today in the workplace. You could encounter a big stop sign and will need to think outside the box to resolve this. Stubborn energy prevents you from moving on so take this time to find a different perspective or remove unattainable and unrealistic goals.

Thursday 13th

Introspection would do you good today. Go within yourself and look at your habitual reactions. Have you outgrown them, or do you still cling on to them because they once helped? It may be time to adapt to a more mature and evolved way of reacting to outside stimuli and triggers.

Friday 14th

Air energy can make your mind exceptionally busy today. Searching your psyche for pearls of wisdom may result in several 'aha!' moments. Revelations stack up and you might kick yourself for not having seen these before. Be good to yourself and learn where your boundaries have been blurred.

Saturday 15th

The early hours may bring vivid dreams and you wake needing to sort fact from fiction. Is it a memory or a dream that has been triggering vulnerable feelings within you? You may need help to answer this question and your family of birth may provide the answers. Nurture your inner child.

Sunday 16th

Today you can be protective or defensive of your own environment. If you need to stay in your shell and take a day off, gather nourishing resources and feed your soul with things you love to do. Nobody will blame you for having a day of quality time to yourself.

Monday 17th

Starting the working week may seem like a burden as you could still be feeling vulnerable and may not wish to be exposed. Your inner compass doesn't seem to be working and you may feel lost. Under this influence, you may feel attacked or manipulated. Watch out for passive-aggressive behaviour.

Tuesday 18th

Your voice returns and you could be feeling stronger today. Keep your inner fire burning and stand up for yourself. Self-expression in the workplace could go two ways, so ensure that what you need to say is true, respectful and kind. You could use defensiveness or self-righteousness to cope.

Wednesday 19th

It's possible that you're at the other end of the scale since the weekend. You could be brash and obnoxious in order to cover up your perceived weaknesses. People will see through this as it isn't the real you. Watch out for clashes with your social groups. Especially the leaders.

Thursday 20th

A change of mood and energy might bring you back to your normal self. It could be that a friend or family member has reminded you who you are and that you are cherished for being authentic. You could feel silly for being stroppy or childish when wanting your own way.

Friday 21st

An energetically quiet day may allow you to come back to your centre and ground yourself. Practical activities which need thorough mental processes would be good for you. Filing, sorting, administration or decluttering will help take your mind off any recent worries and lift your self-esteem. Keep yourself occupied this way.

Saturday 22nd

Stay away from dreaming or attempting to find your inner compass. Today is needed for essential maintenance of your body. Make a medical appointment if you've been neglecting your health recently. You may need a tonic, but for now, a walk in nature or physical exercise will suffice.

Sunday 23rd

Saturn turns direct today and will ease some of the pressure in your intimate relationships. You might have learned some valuable lessons about boundaries this year. The next few weeks are about to get creative and seductive, so you may wish to practise maintaining healthy boundaries even more now.

Monday 24th

Your head and heart are in sync and you might feel much more balanced. Your rational and logical side matches your emotions and brings a sense of calm. A fresh new perspective on relating to deep levels can be exciting and you are eager to explore what this means for you.

Tuesday 25th

A new moon and a solar eclipse open a window of wild card energy. This can be intimate and exotic, and you may need to keep your wits about you. As Venus is also involved, this will almost certainly involve romance or creative projects. Stay grounded as you could fall madly in love.

Wednesday 26th

A shock or a ghost from the past could visit and you will need to deal with it once and for all. Be firm but fair and throw the past back to where it belongs. This may be your first chance to exercise a strong boundary and say no.

Thursday 27th

Stay alert and be mindful that you could be prone to illusions now. You could be charmed into believing that a euphoric state is the real thing when it may just be a lovely drug. Get out and do your mundane duties and take your mind off romance for now.

Friday 28th

Your sense of joy and optimism could be disguised as something else right now. If you experience a big pull into spiritual enlightenment, stay safe as this could also be an illusion. Travel and the exotic attract you now, but are not really options. Be satisfied with documentaries and research.

Saturday 29th

It's possible that you've been knocked off course and could be asking for a lifeboat to get back to shore. You may have bitten off more than you can chew. Be humble and ask for the help you need to reorient yourself. A trusted friend or partner can help.

Sunday 30th

Mars turns retrograde now. This will occur in your most private thoughts and you may have a period of slowing down your internal progress. Use it as a rest stop and enjoy the break. Partner time can be sensual and delightful without all the high romance, music and poetry.

Monday 31st

If you need a little help staying in control and grounded, look to a partner. You might find that they are happy to help if it means they have you on planet Earth for a while. Enjoy a time of shared visions and discuss how the two of you can change the world together.

NOVEMBER

. . . .

Tuesday 1st

Challenges persist and you could be too scared to make a move for fear of disrupting the status quo. The best thing you can do today is to accept and understand your responsibilities towards groups. Change and progress are being made with or without your contribution.

Wednesday 2nd

Go within and find an anchor as you might feel out of your depth today. Just be sure that this isn't an addiction or coping mechanism which is unhealthy. A matter regarding love and romance may need to be dealt with. Is this a ghost from the past that needs banishing?

Thursday 3rd

Fluid energy can make you adaptable to any circumstance but can also feel ungrounded. The emotional realm is where you work naturally, but this may be an overload. It can be consuming but may also help you move things along and work with the changing currents.

Friday 4th

Your inner compass calls and you have a chance to evaluate recent events. You might change your perspective or decide that something is not in alignment with your core values. Emotions may be bigger than usual, so hold tight and accept this journey as it could be the healing you need.

Saturday 5th

It's important that you let go of things which you're using as an emotional crutch. Learn to see yourself as worthy of good things and let unhealthy habits or behaviours go. This may cause you some inner conflict or problems in your romance, but this is necessary for growth.

Sunday 6th

Be proactive today and make lists of things that can help you at work and also with your inner process. A group of like-minded friends could provide what you need to know now. Difficult conversations are the catalyst for discarding anything that is weighing you down or keeping you from moving on.

Monday 7th

Look for quality now. If you've made space in your life, there's room for something new to come in. Don't pick up the first thing you see. Be discerning and only accept what is offered if it has meaning and can bring you pleasure. Choose something you can treasure.

Tuesday 8th

You might feel a pull towards a bright future which has solid roots. A full moon and lunar eclipse close the wild card window of energy. You may feel this strongly and should be passive and let it play out. It could be that something has been removed from your life forever.

Wednesday 9th

Clear up any debris from recent events. You might hear or speak harsh words today and this could upset you. A new cycle is starting and is activated by energy which penetrates and destroys. There is a creative way you can use this energy and you will work this out soon.

Thursday 10th

The gossip line could be busy today as people catch up and make their own versions of events. Ensure you're not the one spreading it. Allow yourself to settle into something creative which is in line with your personal path. This may be dreamy and poetic.

Friday 11th

You could experience a mental block, and this could irritate you. Words escape you or are chosen badly and may result in a misunderstanding. You might perceive this as unfair on your part and try rectifying the problem, but you may not get far. Wait until this energy passes.

Saturday 12th

Your ruler, the moon, drops into your sign and you might notice this by an increase in intuition or sensitivity. Your hopes, dreams and romantic pursuits can be easily communicated now. It could be that you've found a muse or been beguiled by beauty. If you can express it, do so.

Sunday 13th

The earth could shake a little as you feel disturbances around you. These may be exciting and fill you with nervous pleasure. Think of it like a small child waiting for Christmas. You could be on the edge of having everything you've ever wanted. Anticipation is adrenalin for your inner child.

Monday 14th

Seductive energy continues to thrill and fascinate. You could be nourished and soul-fed by romantic and creative activity. Step into your strength and show the world who you are. If you feel like royalty, enjoy the uplift this gives you and notice how much taller you feel.

Tuesday 15th

You could be walking around in a surreal fantasy land. However, you might also be acutely aware and afraid that this could disappear at any moment. A last minute or rushed attempt to enhance your romantic relationships isn't needed. Have confidence that this energy is floating around you for a reason you are yet to understand.

Wednesday 16th

Today you should try to communicate or create something deep and mysterious. This may be uncomfortable for you, but will be the only way you can bring forth what it is you desire. Take a leap of faith and stay true to yourself. Speak without fear.

Thursday 17th

You could be worrying that you've spoken out of turn. Your fear of rejection has you going through everything you've said. Don't analyse this too much as you will find yourself in a muddle. Be open-hearted and offer yourself unconditionally. Trust that you're in the right place at the right time.

Friday 18th

Do something which helps you stay grounded today. Practical or mundane activities can be useful to distract you from your internal worries. This evening you might need to put in extra effort as you could be at risk of wallowing in your own lack of confidence.

Saturday 19th

Your home and family can be the support structure you need right now. There's no need to spill everything that's in your mind or heart, just appreciate that they're there for you. Gentle care and lighthearted conversation can be a tonic and make you feel nurtured. They may also give you courage.

Sunday 20th

Knowing your duties and responsibilities today can be a source of harmony. The world still revolves around natural rhythms and cycles, even though you may feel out of balance. Enjoy family time which can be respectful and soothing to your soul. Your contribution will be valued and appreciated.

Monday 21st

Mark this day as extremely auspicious. You could see everything drop into place nicely and could wonder why you worried so much. Important conversations this evening can touch a deep part of you and inspire you to be brave and bold. Go after what you desire with a passionate heart.

Tuesday 22nd

The cosmic waste bin is waiting for you to drop your unhelpful emotional responses in. You may be reviewing how you've experienced sharing in the past. It could be time to think about your security and make plans to try something new. Take your time as letting go is never easy.

Wednesday 23rd

Today you could be successful and take control in relationship matters. This might mean making changes which can be beneficial and life-changing. The intensity of this can be exhilarating and daunting, but if shared with another, it can also connect the two of you on a deeper level than you can imagine.

Thursday 24th

There is wonderful energy for you to access today. A new moon heralds the start of a brave new journey of unconditional love and duty to another. Jupiter turns direct and will bring bounty to your career. Conversations are easy and love is harmonious and heartfelt.

Friday 25th

You could experience a little setback today, but this will soon pass. This might be from within and may be that voice of self-doubt. It could be that you believe you aren't worthy of good things or that you are swimming out of your depth. Don't jump in at the deep end.

Saturday 26th

An easy weekend awaits you. You might contemplate the past and future together and look at where you're standing now. Sharing, caring, finances and pleasure could all be the issues you think about. What didn't work for you in the past may now have a chance of succeeding.

Sunday 27th

Partner time can bring unexpected delight today. You might notice that your dreams are now founded on Earth, which can sustain you better. Change no longer frightens you. The future looks bright and you can look forward to expanding your world vision. Perhaps a course of study or travel is on the agenda.

Monday 28th

An outgoing mood can make people stop and wonder what has happened to you. Don't let anyone bring you down today, not that they could. You don't need to be supercharged and running around because your good spirits are what is motivating you. Your boundaries are strong and healthy.

Tuesday 29th

Thought processes might be doing overtime today. There may be long-standing problems which you are now slowly figuring out. Digging deep and taking time to understand what you find may be the best way to uncover the gold hidden in your psyche. Seek to learn and share your wisdom.

Wednesday 30th

Floaty energy surrounds you once more. You could have a spiritual epiphany which shows you how far you can go and still feel at home. Conversations can be more intellectual or exploratory. It's possible that you have found a teacher or guru to guide you on the next part of your journey.

DECEMBER

. . . .

Thursday 1st

Keep a level head today as you might come back down to
Earth with a bump. This is a temporary mood, so refrain from
making decisions until you have more clarity of vision. You
can connect with your inner compass but may need a day
alone to process feelings.

Friday 2nd

Try not to talk yourself into, or out of something now. Your
emotions could be off the scale but can also be the impetus
for making a jump into the unknown. However, don't be too
impulsive or impatient. Return to career projects and make
lists and plans.

Saturday 3rd

Gathering resources will show your leadership skills in a good
light. Those in charge may be impressed by what they see of
you today so stick to your duties. You may also show these
qualities in your home life and claim your authority as a good
administrator.

Sunday 4th

Neptune turns direct today. From your inner compass, you
may now have a better direction on where your future lies.
What is no longer important to you will dissolve or fade away.
You might experience this as a new perspective on an old
situation. Plant seeds which have more value to you now.

Monday 5th

Friendship groups could have something new for you today.
There may be a lot of activity with innovative plans going on.
If you want to get involved, you must contribute in some way
which will ensure your part in the team. Quality interactions
can lead to positive action.

Tuesday 6th

You may be in a rush to get a chore done today. Deadlines
could be close and needing your attention. Put your nose
to the grindstone and aim to complete things today. Deep
conversations with a partner are possible and can help you
understand a concept that has been evading you.

Wednesday 7th

Today you have a chance to work at your own pace. This might
be easier for you if unencumbered by outside obligations.
Working alone in an environment free of chatter will help you
focus on the job. Alternatively, you may choose to use today to
review your inner work and progress so far.

Thursday 8th

A full moon may bring you a revelation. Look within yourself
to see what has changed for you this year. You may not have
noticed how much you've grown but the results are there.
Understand that you alone are responsible for changing things
which no longer serve you.

Friday 9th

If you need more time today, ask for it. You could be feeling vulnerable or defensive if people are rushing you. Try to be flexible and stay positive. Don't worry about what others think of you if you need to progress in baby steps or ask a lot of questions.

Saturday 10th

Your relationship zone is blessed with the arrival of Venus. Expect to give and receive more compassion. You might wish to take things slowly and enjoy the journey rather than rush to the next level. Expect the unexpected and go out for some fun with friends to kick off the festive season.

Sunday 11th

You could have vivid dreams and wake thinking about how a partner sees you now. An awareness of the steps you've taken together may overwhelm you until you get a chance to discuss this. Speak your truth and let them know if you have financial concerns.

Monday 12th

The working week begins with putting your heart into your work. You might find more pleasure from doing a job well, even if it takes you longer than expected. Walk tall and be proud that you've given it your best shot. Take time to observe your own work and reward yourself.

Tuesday 13th

Today may be tricky as you may need to push someone's boundaries to get them moving. This isn't meant to hurt them, but it can go against all you've learned this year and it hurts you. Your fast-flowing energy is needed to encourage others to do the same and be productive.

Wednesday 14th

Ground yourself today and get on with practical tasks
which are engaging and time-consuming. There's no time
for dreaming or idle chatter now. Any conversations can
be productive and significant. You may need to ensure that
you read all the details and know how something works to
understand it.

Thursday 15th

Close partnerships can feel the benefit of grounding energy
today. A partner may bring out the best in you and help you be
more practical and less emotional. They can ensure that your
personal growth is being nurtured and nourished properly and
this feeds your Cancerian soul.

Friday 16th

Hopes and dreams need to take a back seat today. You might
feel resentful about this as your heart yearns to merge or
connect with the ethereal energy you've enjoyed recently.
There's work to be done and you need to be thorough. Perhaps
you could do a physical end-of-year clear-out.

Saturday 17th

To be fair to all, you might need to divide your time between
lovers and family. This could tug on the heartstrings a little as
you feel you may be letting someone down. A social gathering
can be interesting this evening if you have time in your busy
social calendar.

Sunday 18th

Today you could have a better idea of how to spend your free time. Prioritising your obligations must come first and then you can leave time to play or relax. You may be pleased with yourself by the end of the day, so treat yourself to something very special.

Monday 19th

The energy is intense now and you must get creative with it. Romantic partners may pull you close and demand more of your attention. This isn't a bad thing unless you lose yourself in the process. Ensure that mind games are not being played as this can hurt your sensitive soul.

Tuesday 20th

High energy can make the air around you electric. This can be volatile or sexy, but either way, you may feel the earth move. You could be putting your foot down and making your own demands as you feel you're being used or manipulated. End anything which is hurting you.

Wednesday 21st

You might have a multitude of chores to do today, but speed and motivation are with you. Perhaps you have deadlines to meet. The winter solstice arrives, and the shortest day gives you added urgency to get things done. Prepare for some cosy time with a partner over the next month.

Thursday 22nd

Love and friendships can bring early surprises today. Stay flexible and be open to invitations. Your diligence when doing mundane tasks meets the approval of elders, but don't overstretch yourself and commit to something which might not be in your best interests. Keep your mind fresh for your own plans.

Friday 23rd

A new moon occurs in your relationship zone and heralds a brand-new start. A project or long-term plan you share with another may seem like hard work but will prove beneficial to you both. This can put a new spin on your relationship or elevate it to another level.

Saturday 24th

Today is filled with anticipation and easy connections. Partner time is highlighted and can be dreamy and loving. You may already feel the effects of a new cycle and look forward to becoming your best self with your dearest. Your intuition tells you that your softness and sensitivity are a bonus.

Sunday 25th

If everything has been prepared, you can enjoy a day of kindness and surprises. This festive day has great planetary energy and you may feel part of something bigger which excites you. Merging and connecting with family and tribe can make you realise how blessed you are.

Monday 26th

It's possible that you're tired and might struggle to fulfil duties today. An event with your social groups may not be as attractive, and declining could be your best option. You might have a good sense of your own limits and save your energy for smaller events closer to home.

Tuesday 27th

Switch off, kick back and do your own thing today. Simply enjoy things which can help you unwind and forget any worries. You may be thinking about holidays or educating yourself about other cultures. Use your free time to research new possibilities. Drift off into your personal fantasy land. No one will mind.

Wednesday 28th

Nicely timed, your inner compass appears, and you check in with yourself. You may be reminiscing about the year gone by. Gratitude and satisfaction fill your heart as you feel perfectly aligned with who you are and who you now want to become. This is growth and you're doing fine.

Thursday 29th

Mercury turns retrograde today. As always, ensure your communications are clear and double-check travel plans. Your heart may be bursting with ideas you would like to put in place in the coming year. Test these out by having discussions with your partner or closest friend.

Friday 30th

You could be swimming against the tide today and feeling a little irritated. Nothing can progress in the holiday season. Don't allow yourself to get into a bad mood just because you want something instantly and it isn't available or possible. Wait this out with grace and patience.

Saturday 31st

Although the daytime could be challenging, try not to cause friction with a partner. There might be an invitation to celebrate with friends this evening and you could enjoy this. Alternatively, a night alone with a partner may see subtle power games going on. Choose wisely.

Cancer

······················

DAILY FORECASTS
for 2023

JANUARY

. . . .

Sunday 1st

The start of a new year is the ideal time to start over. Say goodbye to a relationship, either personal or professional, that's toxic and damages your mental health. Celebrate the new year with a good friend.

Monday 2nd

If you've recently met someone new, it's an ideal time to get to know them better. Don't rush into a relationship; instead, take your time and get to know someone slowly. The right kind of friends will get who you are and support you wholeheartedly. Reach out to other people.

Tuesday 3rd

If you know your mind is lively and you're prone to worry or anxiety, it's important to find ways to relax and be calm. If meditation works for you, make it a regular practice. If you prefer to talk about your feelings or write things down, find what's right for you.

Wednesday 4th

Be more objective and rational in your close relationships. Take a step back and consider the bigger picture and where you're heading as a couple. When you meet the right person, there tends to be a flow and ease of connection. Trust the process both at home and at work.

Thursday 5th

Get the right friends on your side and you can achieve anything. Veer towards the friend who encourages you to be true to yourself and step out of your comfort zone. You may decide to team up with an alternative group of people who have revolutionary and innovative ideas.

Friday 6th

During today's full moon, the spotlight is on you. Trust your emotions and make a clear decision regarding a significant relationship or partnership. You may be on the verge of breaking away from someone who's been in your life for an unusually long time. Experience your feelings deeply.

Saturday 7th

It helps to talk but this isn't the time to try and win someone over or nail an argument. You can chat until the cows come home, but that doesn't mean you'll end up in agreement with them! You'll see one situation more clearly come this month's new moon.

Sunday 8th

It's a lovely day to be generous and treat yourself or your family. You could learn a lot from witnessing another person's actions. This evening, it's worth staying up late to catch up with a good friend.

Monday 9th

When it comes to relationships, you may return to the past in some shape or form. You could hear from an ex, or perhaps you're comparing a current relationship to a loving one from a long time ago. Communication and friendship open the door to an honest and caring connection.

Tuesday 10th

You may feel weighed down by an emotional or financial issue. Be honest about your reality and try not to let fear take hold. You might recognise where you need to cut costs or guard your heart. Talking to a neighbour or sibling will help you put the world to rights.

Wednesday 11th

It seems as if there's a lot to talk about right now. You might be keen to set up a strong support network close to home. Alternatively, you may be dealing with an ongoing personal issue that began a few months ago. Be proactive and do what's necessary to get your questions answered.

Thursday 12th

If you've been through a dark and difficult journey over the last few months, this is the time for you to engage with what's up ahead. Confront whatever's challenging you and be assertive in your approach to life. Deal with any secrets or demons head-on and start by being honest.

Friday 13th

Trust your instincts when it comes to love. You know a relationship is right for you when you don't have to say anything, and you feel comfortable in the other person's presence. Create space to be with your family or spend more time at home over the weekend.

Saturday 14th

If you're typical of your star sign, your home is your haven. You benefit when you have somewhere you can retreat to where you feel comfortable and safe. It's a lovely day to spend money on your home, or get together with family members and do something special.

Sunday 15th

You might be trying something different when it comes to your love life. Anything goes, whether you're in a 'friends with benefits' liaison or you're going out with someone who's not your usual type. There is an unpredictable edge to love today so be ready for drama or the unexpected.

Monday 16th

Your love life could be exciting or infuriating today – definitely not boring or mundane. You may be the one chasing someone new, or perhaps you have an admirer who will make their feelings known. A child might need you for a heart-to-heart.

Tuesday 17th

Don't turn a blind eye to finances today. Ensure you open your bills or check your bank balance. You may experience disappointment around money, but try to be realistic about what you can and can't afford.

Wednesday 18th

Talk planet Mercury turns direct in your relationship zone today. A conversation may be challenging but the time is right to speak up. If you feel under pressure from your boss or a powerful individual, set firm boundaries in place or take a step back if necessary.

Thursday 19th

Keep your eye on the prize and take whatever steps help you remain focused. You may be easily distracted or lose yourself daydreaming today. It might help to think of the money at work and line up some long-term goals. This evening, be with the one you love and lean on each other.

Friday 20th

It's an important weekend to regain some balance in your personal life. Start by looking at your situation objectively or discuss what's going on with an outsider, someone you're not personally involved with. Be open-minded and write things down if you have a lot going on.

Saturday 21st

Today's new moon in Aquarius highlights one of the hidden zones of your horoscope. It's a good time to get to grips with taboo issues or anything that's been challenging you of late. Get on top of money matters and pay close attention to any shared resources.

Sunday 22nd

It's not easy if you're only dealing with serious issues in a relationship and love has become more practical than romantic. Take stock if this is true for you. Where you can be sure of excitement is in your friendships, although anything goes lately, so it could get crazy and wild.

Monday 23rd

You may be dealing with loss or grief. Be kind to yourself if you're more emotional than usual and your feelings run deep. Sometimes, it helps to have a good cry as this can act as a release. Do whatever feels right for you.

Tuesday 24th

You could find your thoughts running away with you today, but it's important to put the brakes on if necessary. If you keep worrying about a situation, it could eventually turn into paranoia. Reach out to the person who knows how to ground you and keep you sane.

Wednesday 25th

A wave of good fortune is boosting your career and finances. Be expansive and hold on to what's possible rather than limit your options. If you hear of a job or project that could take you overseas, find out more. It's an ideal day to believe in your hopes and dreams.

Thursday 26th

The planet of opportunity is in your career and vocation zone. Make a wish and set new ideas or plans in motion. It's hard to change anything in your life unless you're prepared to take a risk and you have a strong sense of self-belief. Hold on to your vision for your future path.

Friday 27th

Today's stars are about escape and using your dreams or imagination to find an escape from the everyday. Music, film, poetry or art could be your muse. You might be planning a holiday or a weekend trip away, or losing yourself in a good book or movie.

Saturday 28th

Try not to get caught up with chores or mundane matters this weekend. You need a break and a chance to do something different. If you're visiting friends in a different part of the country, you're in tune with your stars. Don't let money hold you back – live your life to the full.

Sunday 29th

Take a break from your normal routine and hang out with some new friends. Being around people who have a different lifestyle can be invigorating and help you see an alternative to your current situation. Group activities are well-starred so make sure you join in.

Monday 30th

If you want to bring something new to a long-term relationship, it would be a good date to talk about meeting new friends together. Make plans to socialise or join a club or society where you share a mutual interest. If you're single, love and friendship go hand in hand.

Tuesday 31st

Take care that you don't turn angry thoughts in on yourself. You could consider talking to a therapist or choose to line up more support in another way. Sometimes, all it takes is naming what's troubling you to start the process of recovery. Dig deep to reveal more.

FEBRUARY

· · · · · · · · · · · · · · · · · ·

Wednesday 1st

It's not the easiest of days, especially if you're the worrying sort. Learn tips and tricks to help slow down your busy mind and make an extra effort to be kind to yourself. Trying to get a lot done could feel impossible, so give yourself a break and do less, not more.

Thursday 2nd

The Moon is back in your star sign and you're likely to feel more emotionally stable. Put your needs first and don't fall into the trap of trying to please everyone else before yourself, especially in the office. Plan a holiday or trip away with the one you love.

Friday 3rd

There may be certain things that you don't want to hear right now. If so, let another person know that you're not ready to talk. You may need a break from reality so line up a trip to the cinema or drinks with friends. Step outside the everyday and do something magical.

Saturday 4th

Now's the time to get on top of your life admin. If you've been considering a financial overview, make it happen or turn to an expert for good advice. Be wary of taking a big risk but keep up to date with the important stuff.

Sunday 5th

Today's full moon is significant for you because, as a Sun Cancer, you're the moonchild of the zodiac. This full moon feels emotional, but also fun and joyful. It's about money for you, so think about treating yourself or the ones you love. You may receive a gift or generous act.

Monday 6th

Start the week as you mean to go on and adopt a positive attitude. Being around people who inspire your dreams can encourage you to keep your eye on the future and your next steps. You don't have to put up with negativity.

Tuesday 7th

It's a good day for keeping busy without being a busybody. If you're typical of your star sign, you love to find out the latest gossip and know what the neighbours are up to. Enjoy yourself in your local neighbourhood without becoming overly embroiled in other people's business.

Wednesday 8th

If you're looking for something more today, reach out to friends who live abroad or live an alternative lifestyle. The more you open yourself up to diversity and variety, the more interested and engaged you become in life. Be willing to experiment when it comes to love.

Thursday 9th

If you were up late talking with your other half or someone close, take it easy today. You benefit from a laid-back vibe and a harmonious environment. Ideally, you'll be at home staying cosy. If you're at work, make an extra effort to get on with other people.

Friday 10th

You may be up against a tough competitor or have someone in your life who doesn't do what you want. You might be questioning what other people mean to you, and aware that some conversations are more damaging than helpful. If so, it could be time to say no.

Saturday 11th

Talk planet Mercury moves into your finance zone today, so it might be time to talk money. The more in touch you are with the technological world, the more likely you are to do well. Keep up to date with all the latest trends.

Sunday 12th

It's an ideal day to focus on pleasure and do more of what you love. If you're in a relationship, make time for love and intimacy. If you're ready for romance, let someone know. Be clear about your motivations, however, and don't lead a friend on if you're not that interested.

Monday 13th

Your romance zone is under lucky stars, but you'd be wise to be smart about the decisions you make rather than fall too deeply too fast. Some objectivity or rational thinking could stop you from making a fool of yourself. Steer clear of a potential lover who can't show their emotions.

Tuesday 14th

This could turn out to be a lovely day for your work or career. If there's an opportunity to get in front of someone in a position of influence, use your charm and make sure you're noticed. Work on your elevator pitch if you don't have long to make a good impression.

Wednesday 15th

Give yourself space to dream and visualise what's next for you. This is especially important if you know you have some big decisions to make over the next few months. It's an ideal time to expand your world and you benefit from seeking inspiration. Love and romance peak at lunchtime.

Thursday 16th

If you have an important conversation or negotiation this week, take it seriously. Do your preparation, consider all eventualities, and don't leave any rock unturned. It's a big week for money decisions and considering your financial security. Get the support you need.

Friday 17th

Relationships are like mirrors and can reflect the parts of yourself that you like and don't like. Today, you'll enjoy being around someone who sees into your soul and brings out a different side of your personality. Be around people who inspire you in all areas of life.

Saturday 18th

Think of your life as a journey, as this is the best way to use the Sun's move into Pisces today. Take yourself off somewhere new, consider your beliefs and your spiritual path, and say yes to any weird or wonderful invitations that come your way. Actively seek adventure and new experiences.

Sunday 19th

As you're one of the emotional water signs, you benefit from soulmate connections in love and friendship. Being around people who help you tap into the depth of your emotions can be healing as well as romantic. Encourage your other half to connect with you on a deep level.

Monday 20th

Today's new moon means it's a good date to set your intentions and try something new. It doesn't matter if it leads you nowhere; what's important is that you're open to new thoughts, ideas and emotions. Step outside of your comfort zone and expand your experience of life.

Tuesday 21st

Pay close attention to the people you meet at the start of this week. This is important regarding your career and vocation and the role you play out in the world. Make the right connections and expand your network. Attract an influencer or role model to harness your success.

Wednesday 22nd

Don't hold back at work today. Instead, engage in a full-on charm offensive and aim to get the right people on your side. It could be an excellent day to boost your popularity and win support. When you have the right team behind you, nothing can stop you.

Thursday 23rd

The spotlight remains on your career and where you're heading in life. If there's a chance to boost your status or improve your reputation, don't hesitate to act. The bigger you play in life, the more chance you have of gaining a first place or winning the top prize.

Friday 24th

An early morning meeting may not bring about the desired results. Only get up early if you know it's going to be worth your while. You may be keen to let your friends know what's been happening this week and who you've been talking to, so arrange a social get-together later on.

. . . .

Saturday 25th

It's possible to keep your excitement levels high today if you involve your friends in what's going on in your life. If you've recently met someone who's made a big impact on you, let your friends know and get to relive the joy all over again.

Sunday 26th

A community event would be the ideal way to spend your Sunday, so consider getting involved with a group of volunteers in your local neighbourhood. Later on, you may sense that you're peopled out and need some quiet time to recharge your batteries.

Monday 27th

Use social media to win friends and influence people today. You might have something to say, or perhaps you're proud of your achievements and want to share your glory. Be careful not to brag, however, and keep your intentions modest and humble.

Tuesday 28th

You might be feeling tired or low in energy today, especially if you were overthinking and couldn't sleep. Try not to take on too much, but turn to other people to help you, whether you delegate at work or get some extra support at home.

MARCH
·················

Wednesday 1st

It's an ideal day to revisit your personal goals and reconsider your image. It's all about how you come across to other people. Be true to who you are today and speak from the heart. You can trust your emotions to guide you.

Thursday 2nd

Today's stars could flag up an award, achievement or promotion. Your connections may prove to be a positive influence for giving, receiving and widening your horizons. Seek new opportunities and show off your skills and talents. It's your turn in the cosmic spotlight.

Friday 3rd

Today is gorgeous for dreams and vision work, for seeking inspiration and beauty in life. Book a holiday or find out more about a course, new experience or project – anything that motivates you. If you're in a relationship, it could be a good time to line up a solo adventure.

Saturday 4th

If you've been doing well financially, this might be a lovely day to treat yourself and the ones you love. Splash out on something special, then, each time you look at what you bought, you'll remember how proud you felt.

Sunday 5th

Rather than overthink things, take action. If there's something you know you've been putting off, today would be a good day to tackle it. Once you start, you may be surprised by how easy it is and how quickly you get it done. Adopt the mantra, 'just do it'.

Monday 6th

If you're planning something momentous, be careful who you choose to tell. If you know someone close has a history of dampening your hopes, turn your attentions elsewhere. Focus on strengthening your purpose as an antidote to fear.

Tuesday 7th

If you're itching to get away and travel, or you want to embark on a new study project, you're in tune with your stars. Live life to the full. Move away from the ordinary towards the extraordinary. It's a good day to sign up for a workshop or focus on your personal development.

Wednesday 8th

When it comes to your long-term hopes and dreams, it could help to draw up a realistic plan. Work slowly and steadily towards your future goals and don't worry if you only take one small step at a time. It's an ideal period for ideas, research and study.

Thursday 9th

You don't have to prove anything to anyone. You might want to try to persuade a family member that you're doing the right thing, but it's more important to convince yourself. Life is urging you to say yes to the wheel of fortune and get on board with your big plans.

Friday 10th

If there's someone at work who sees your potential and is encouraging you to step into a new role or position of responsibility, take note. Sometimes, other people see what we can't see in ourselves. Don't miss out on a new opportunity.

Saturday 11th

The lovers of the heavens are working in unison today, but it's more of a professional than a personal vibe. If you're looking for a new job or work opportunity, use your people skills and reach out to others. Someone from your past could help you seal a deal.

Sunday 12th

If you want more fun and entertainment in your life, find the right people to join you. If you're in a relationship, convince your other half to get on board. If you're single, turn to an adventurous friend and line up something exciting together. Don't waste your life sitting on the sofa.

Monday 13th

If you don't enjoy your current job or role in life, you might feel as if you're missing out. However, rather than feeling bad about what's happening, explore your options outside of work or your daily routine. Try and change your attitude from 'live to work' to 'work to live'.

Tuesday 14th

Be wary of other people's motives today as someone may be out to hurt or shame you. Don't trust everyone you meet under these elusive stars. This is about karma and being responsible for past actions. This could apply to you or someone close.

Wednesday 15th

Be savvy at work and ask other people to help you. You may feel under pressure if there's something you want to achieve but you could be up against strong opposition. Talk to your other half at lunchtime and stay up late to pursue a personal wish or dream.

Thursday 16th

Other people could be causing you hassle and you may need to keep a tight hold on your temper. Admittedly, they might be getting cross at you because you're finding it hard to concentrate. Reach out to a dear friend this evening for good times and support.

Friday 17th

Be careful around someone who hurts you today. Whatever you say could be wrong and whatever you try to get excited about, they put down. Your personal relationships could be more volatile than usual, whereas your oldest friendships are solid and a strong anchor in your life.

Saturday 18th

If you're feeling hurt or vulnerable, you may feel better once you've said your piece. You might ideally like to resolve a personal difficulty, but don't expect too much today. Instead, turn to the people in your life you know you can rely on to be there for you, whatever happens.

Sunday 19th

Talk planet Mercury enters your career zone, so gear up and get ready for a busy couple of weeks. Work on your confidence levels as this is a good time to be bold and courageous. Once you start talking about something that excites you, you might find it hard to stop.

Monday 20th

The Sun's move into Aries today heralds the equinox, an ideal date for a reset, a fresh start. Aries is the star sign at the peak of your horoscope. Think about your career, your vocation and your future path. Be proactive in deciding where you're heading and why.

Tuesday 21st

It's a good week to think about your vocation in life and what's next for you. You may already be contemplating new ideas or be weighing up new opportunities. Today's new moon is an ideal date to set some new intentions.

Wednesday 22nd

This would be a great time to launch a project or take on a new position or role. Aries' energy is innovative and trendsetting. You're one of the cardinal star signs, which means you slip easily into a leadership role. This might be at home or out in the world, but both are equally significant.

Thursday 23rd

A cycle comes to completion today and this could coincide with a momentous shift in a personal relationship. You might be considering a new future with someone, or be ready to move away from a partnership that's dominated your life for over a decade.

Friday 24th

Celebrate with good friends and enjoy your social life. If you're looking for love, get out and about and ask for introductions. There's a fun, spontaneous vibe to your astrology, so it's an ideal day to say yes to a last-minute invitation. Life is a rollercoaster – enjoy the ride!

Saturday 25th

It's taken a long time, but action planet Mars finally enters your star sign today. This is an ambitious influence that promises passion but potentially arguments too. You may be ready and raring to go, especially if you've felt bored or held back lately.

Sunday 26th

Mars' move into your star sign can feel like an adrenalin rush, a time when you're ready to embrace your daredevil nature and be bold and courageous. You could decide to bungee-jump, ride a fast sports car or unleash your inner rebel. Whatever you do, make it wild.

Monday 27th

You could benefit from less distraction today if you've got a lot of tasks lined up. Switch off your phone and engage with other people face-to-face. One-to-one connections could make a big difference to your work and career goals.

Tuesday 28th

An early morning meeting or interview gets the thumbs up. It might be hard to wake up early, but it's worth it if you hear the news you've been waiting for. Whatever you're involved with, don't let fear take hold. Fake it until you make it. The stars are on your side.

Wednesday 29th

Being one of the water signs, you have natural instincts and empathy with other people. Use these skills today as you can read other people well. Be compassionate and caring. Reaching out to a good friend could have a bigger impact than you may imagine. Trust your emotions.

Thursday 30th

Love and friendship are linked today, which is great news if you're ready to meet someone special. There may be a connection to someone who lives abroad, or a person you know from school or a study course. Don't be shy; let someone close know how you feel.

Friday 31st

Your confidence around other people could rub off on them. Dare to take centre stage and lead others, especially in a work environment. If you're looking for a raise or you're keen on applying for promotion, set the wheels of success in motion.

APRIL
· · · · · · · · · · · · · · · · ·

Saturday 1st

This could turn out to be a powerful month for you. Don't be an April fool; instead, set some bold intentions around your career and future path. Your star sign is one of the leaders of the zodiac. Create a strong family network around yourself, both personally and professionally.

Sunday 2nd

New ideas may surface when you create more space in your life and take yourself out of your normal routine. Early morning can be a creative time, so do something different – go for a walk or have a leisurely bath or shower. Later on, you may have to verbally defend yourself.

Monday 3rd

It could be a testing day. Someone's decision may sound like an emphatic 'no', but this isn't the end of the story by any means. Political differences or opposing belief systems could challenge you.

Tuesday 4th

Talk planet Mercury will be in your friendship and group zone until mid-June. Your friends are there to lean on and can be a rock for you. If you want to talk to someone about work, love or any other area of your life, choose a trusted confidante – perhaps the person you've known longest.

Wednesday 5th

You can learn a lot from your friends. Ultimately, you need to know where you can turn for support; you might be trying to call in a few favours and it would be wise to do so. It's not the time to start lending or borrowing money.

Thursday 6th

You are the moonchild of the zodiac, which means you often feel the full moon more intensely than other people. Be aware that emotions will be heightened and tempers could flare. Today's full moon could prove to be a significant turning point for your future path.

Friday 7th

It's a good time to find your muse: something beyond yourself that inspires you and gives you faith in life. This is not the time to wallow in your emotions or waste too much energy feeling hard done by. Instead, say yes to life and commit to following your passion.

Saturday 8th

It's an excellent day to walk your talk and take a leading role within a circle of friends or a group context. Being around other people who care for you and you for them will make the long weekend extra special. It might be time to ditch someone who's continually unreliable.

Sunday 9th

Step back and move beyond a partnership that holds you back and doesn't allow you to grow. Instead, lean on your good friends: the people who get you and help you feel more secure and comfortable in your skin. Be true to who you are.

Monday 10th

It may be Easter Monday, but you could be keen to get organised. This might mean you're sorting out the house or dealing with administration and correspondence, or perhaps you're working the holiday shift. Tidying up your surroundings could help to declutter your mind.

Tuesday 11th

Today's Sun-Jupiter connection feels especially fortunate for you. This might be the time when you're rewarded for your efforts, whether you hear about a new job, an opportunity to work abroad, or you're asked to teach, present or share your experiences. Play big in life.

Wednesday 12th

Love planet Venus is in the most private zone of your horoscope for the next few weeks. You could start an affair or fall for someone, but you have to keep your thoughts or feelings private. Talk to someone you trust if you're ready to leap in.

Thursday 13th

It's important to take good care of yourself, especially if you're becoming fearful about current events or what's taking place out in the world. If you're a typical Cancer, you like to feel safe and secure, so it's important to put smart strategies in place if you feel anxious.

Friday 14th

Take it slow when it comes to relationships. It would be easy for you to get hurt especially if you're feeling vulnerable. You may not be confident of your feelings, or you could be caught up in a love triangle. Make sure you know the difference between love and lust.

Saturday 15th

It's a good day to get together with a female colleague or friend to help each other out. Money and work are linked today and there's a social vibe. You might be fundraising or have some great ideas on how to boost your income.

Sunday 16th

If you're feeling bored, a quick way to raise your spirits is to say yes to an adventure or new experience. Do something liberating or adrenalin-seeking. Step out of your comfort zone and initiate an exciting new plan, project or activity. The ball's in your court.

Monday 17th

If you're self-employed, make sure you create some space in your diary to focus on your hopes and dreams. Creativity and new ideas rise more easily to the surface when you step back from your everyday activities. Set some new intentions around where you're heading and why.

Tuesday 18th

This could out to be an important week for you. Not everything will play out as expected, but it could be the start of a new two-year chapter that revolutionises your career or future path. If you're ready for something new, set the wheels in motion and reorient your compass.

Wednesday 19th

This is not the time to hold back, so line up some audacious goals for the rest of 2023 and beyond. It's a good week to dream about the future and where you want to be in 10 years' time. Visualise where you're heading and bring your dreams to life.

Thursday 20th

Events this week could turn out to be a major turning point, thanks to today's solar eclipse at the peak of your horoscope. If something big is bubbling away, you're right to be excited and to take advantage of a new opportunity. Look out for a sign that guides you.

Friday 21st

If you already know this is likely to be a big month for you career-wise, get ready. It could be 'all change' as a new direction in life opens up for you. Mercury's retrograde phase impacts your friendships and it's here where misunderstandings or miscommunications could occur.

Saturday 22nd

If it's been a big week with some significant events taking place, take a step back this weekend. You may be shocked by what's happened or be doubting yourself. Either way, it's an ideal couple of days for rest and retreat. Meditate, relax and slow down your mind.

Sunday 23rd

If you want to explore a new relationship or an attraction that you can't let go of, today would be ideal to reach out and make a connection. There may be something in your life that you're wise to keep private or to yourself. Be careful who you trust as a confidante.

Monday 24th

This could be a powerful chapter to manifest what you want. Aim to stay optimistic and philosophical. Boost your potential with positive thinking and bold actions. Whatever you dream up today could have a positive effect on your finances.

Tuesday 25th

Today, you could be delighted when an old friend reaches out and offers their help or support. You may realise that you have some very different friendships in your life, not all of them close. Don't let your most loyal friendships drift; play your part in them.

Wednesday 26th

Life may be teaching you to trust yourself more or take responsibility for your actions. If you're true to your star sign, you often need reassurance or to reach out for guidance. Recognising that it's up to you how your life plays out can be scary or a blessing. Choose wisely.

Thursday 27th

Pay close attention to finances today, especially if you've been letting things drift recently. You may need to make a tough choice or tighten your belt. You can sometimes compare yourself detrimentally to other people, but try not to do so if possible – it won't be helpful to anyone.

Friday 28th

It's not wise to take financial advice from your friends now. Until Mercury turns direct in mid-May, it's hard to know what's true and what's not. You may discover that you're in a better place in a few more weeks.

Saturday 29th

A moment of insight or illumination could help you win support from someone in an influential position. Being cheeky and asking for a favour can sometimes pay off and work out well. If you're looking for fun, join a new group around town. Today's astrology is great for online dating.

Sunday 30th

Put any disappointments to one side and make a positive effort to get on with the day. It's a good day to socialise and meet up with other people rather than be on your own. This is important if you sense that your emotions are strong and could potentially overwhelm you.

MAY

· · · · · · · · · · · · · · · · ·

Monday 1st

You should be cautious around money, especially joint investments and financial transactions. Today's events could flag up an extreme situation regarding your finances and require you to act decisively. There may be a chance to get rid of a contract or partnership that isn't working out.

Tuesday 2nd

If you're dealing with loss, do your best to ensure your security and let go of anything that's not going well. Most importantly, get support from another family member and don't try to handle everything on your own.

Wednesday 3rd

As a Sun Cancer, it's important that your home life is harmonious and a place you can retreat to. If your home is currently noisy or your family are being argumentative, this won't help your peace of mind. Aim to sort out any disputes or inconveniences as swiftly as you can.

Thursday 4th

This could be a deep and meaningful time for your one-to-ones and there may be an opportunity to reconnect with someone in your life or experience a soulmate encounter. You might be addressing your sex life even if you find it hard to be honest about what you want.

Friday 5th

Don't avoid what you're feeling during today's lunar eclipse. Even your most hidden emotions may come to the surface. It's a powerful eclipse for committing, whether this involves a child, a lover or a creative project. Be aware that eclipses can coincide with endings too.

Saturday 6th

Your emotions ebb and flow like the tide. This means that life with you is rarely boring as you can switch from funny to sad in a nanosecond. Watch out for intense emotions possibly surfacing today, whether you're passionate, jealous or somewhere in between.

Sunday 7th

The planet of love, Venus, enters your star sign today, where it remains for the next few weeks. A private love affair could become public, or perhaps you feel ready to declare your feelings or affections. Line up a date for Tuesday or Wednesday this week.

Monday 8th

Your nature is kind and giving and sometimes you give too much. Re-establish healthy relationships and friendships in your life now. Ensure that your closest relationships are mutually supportive and you're around people who feed your soul. Pay close attention to love.

Tuesday 9th

This would be an ideal time to try out a new online group, especially a network of people who are alternative and unconventional. You may be drawn towards working with younger people, either as a mentor, teacher or coach.

Wednesday 10th

It's important that you stand up for yourself today and don't let other people walk all over you. Be assertive and direct even in your most intimate relationships. If you're always putting out a loved one's fires, encourage them to solve their own problems rather than stepping in to fix things for them.

Thursday 11th

The tidier your financial situation, the better. If you've been holding off on a big purchase, Monday 15th is the turning point, but you might consider how you could cut costs on it or lower expenses.

Friday 12th

Someone from your past could reappear in your life this weekend, perhaps an old flame or someone you knew when you were growing up. It's a good weekend to revisit your memories or to go somewhere different. Shake up your routine a little.

Saturday 13th

If you want to widen your circle of friends, today is a good day to reach out to others. You're at your most attractive with lovely Venus in your star sign, which can help boost your popularity. Alternatively, hanging out with your oldest friends could be the perfect tonic.

Sunday 14th

Work your charm on other people. There's a social vibe today, and being around people who broaden your sphere of influence could be exciting and invigorating. If there's someone you want to talk to who's been absent from your life recently, make the first move and reach out.

Monday 15th

Talk planet Mercury turns direct in your friendship zone today. This would be a good time to sort out a misunderstanding with a friend or make a clear decision about your participation within a group, club or society. Practise forgiveness and dreams can come true.

Tuesday 16th

Jupiter enters your friendship zone today. This is less about doing your own thing at work and more about teaming up with people of influence. You can't do it all on your own moving forward – in fact, you'd be wrong to try. Together, you're bigger and better.

Wednesday 17th

New opportunities come your way when you broaden your horizons, learn from other people and share what you know. Line up a fun new group, online or offline, that can help take you closer towards your chosen goals. Get your friends involved too.

. . . .

Thursday 18th

Consider where or how you can influence others and notice where you're being called to step into a leadership role, especially within society or your community. Avoid friends or groups which leave you feeling down. This is important as you're super sensitive to other people's emotions.

Friday 19th

The friendship zone of your horoscope is extra lively. This is partly due to today's new moon, which heralds a new phase. You may be hanging out with a new group of friends. Alternatively, you could feel ready to move away from a group, club or society.

Saturday 20th

Financial matters are zinging once action planet Mars enters your money zone today. You could be looking into a new money-making project or feel more confident about your ability to take charge and be financially independent. Reassess what you value most highly in your life.

Sunday 21st

If you want to improve your financial affairs, you may first have to cut ties with an organisation or cancel a deal that's doing you no favours. Identify where your money is disappearing into a black hole, then take decisive action to remedy your situation.

Monday 22nd

Think about where you may have gone wrong in the past regarding a financial or emotional issue. It's important not to give yourself a hard time and place all the blame on yourself. That's not to say you should blame someone else, but view the situation objectively.

Tuesday 23rd

Take care not to be overly impulsive today. You might be tempted to help someone out financially, but ensure your heart and head are in alignment before you leap in. Be around the person you love the most and line up a lunchtime date.

Wednesday 24th

If you want to take a step back and engage less actively with life, this fits your current astrology. Sometimes, it's best to put yourself first, especially if you feel unsettled or anxious. Do whatever's necessary to feel more stable.

Thursday 25th

There's a strong focus on the most private zone of your horoscope. It's a good day to consider your feelings without sharing them with everyone concerned. You might be fast learning about yourself, and your personal growth or development could skyrocket.

Friday 26th

If you're looking for love, it's an excellent date to start a conversation, talk to other people and create a spark. If online dating's your thing, you could have some successful matches. Practise random acts of kindness and help to make the world a better place.

Saturday 27th

The wider your circle of friends, the more chance you have of meeting a new love interest. If you're keen to couple up, ask your closest friends for an introduction. If someone criticises you or constantly puts you down, you're right to question why you stay with them.

Sunday 28th

Make sure that you set firm boundaries with other people in your life for the sake of your health and wellbeing. If you're currently caring for someone, perhaps a parent or older person, it's important that you make time for yourself too. Ask for support as and when you need it.

Monday 29th

Someone could let you down today and forget you were meant to be meeting up. Rather than being disappointed, make the most of a change of plan and spend some quality time with your family. There's a possibility that you'll get to know a family member on a much deeper level.

Tuesday 30th

If you're struggling with a personal issue, reach out to someone close. Today's stars confirm that a problem shared is a problem halved when you're honest and open about what you're feeling and share your experiences with loved ones.

Wednesday 31st

You may experience a difference of opinion with someone in your family today. Perhaps you don't approve of their relationship, or they might disapprove of who you're seeing. Rather than letting it come between you, accept one another's differences before it becomes a problem.

JUNE
. . . .

Thursday 1st
You could be embroiled in another person's dramas today, perhaps those of a friend, child or lover. There's a passionate and lively vibe but emotions could run high. Some days, you're wise to live in the present, but keep your gaze firmly set on future goals today.

Friday 2nd
Love is in the air, so make the most of it and line up a date or rendezvous. Wear your heart on your sleeve in a close relationship and let someone know how much you care. If in doubt, put romance first and friendship second. Your feelings count the most.

Saturday 3rd
Create some space in your life this weekend to be quiet so you can listen to your subconscious. Relax, retreat, take a break and rethink your next steps. Try not to get overly caught up in work or chores during this full moon weekend. Tap into your inner voice instead.

Sunday 4th
Today's full moon may highlight where change is necessary, whether this is about your work and routine, your lifestyle or your health. Focus on the basics of life and get these right before you start anything new. Adopt new, healthy habits and create some beneficial rules to live by.

Monday 5th

Keep coming back to the basics, to facts and common sense this week. You're likely to be juggling a lot of balls, so it's up to you to decide which ones are worth holding on to and which you can let go of. This applies to money in particular.

Tuesday 6th

You're stronger when you have the right allies on your side. It's a good day to work on your relationships, both personal and professional. Listen to what your friends have to say and get some expert advice. This might be particularly relevant regarding finances or a legal case.

Wednesday 7th

You could find yourself coming under pressure today, perhaps from someone who's super persuasive, like a salesperson. This could be linked to finance. Don't give in to someone in a position of power or control if you're not sure about their motivations.

Thursday 8th

This may be the time for you to recognise your power and take control of your life and your destiny. You can sometimes come across as weak or vulnerable, but this isn't true. Like your zodiac symbol, the crab, you have a soft underbelly and a tough exterior. Play to your strengths.

Friday 9th

If you've been keeping feelings for a friend to yourself for the last couple of months, tonight could present you with an opportunity to open up and declare your affections. If you say nothing, you will never find out if your feelings are reciprocated. It's an ideal evening for talking love.

Saturday 10th

If you need something to look forward to, make it happen, even if you only take small steps this weekend. It can be easy to compare your own life to the lives of other people, but comparison alone won't change anything. Steer clear of a friend who drives your envy.

Sunday 11th

There's a possibility that you're going to return to an unhealthy situation. If this is because you're lacking closure and you need one final conversation, go for it. If you're giving into temptation and going back to a toxic relationship, however, nip it in the bud rather than giving in.

Monday 12th

If you've been overly indulgent with your spending recently, today is excellent for starting over and setting new intentions around work and finances. Ditch a bad habit, be kind to yourself and banish any inner demons. Silence your critics and crack on with the task at hand.

Tuesday 13th

It's important to stop now and then to take stock of where you're heading and why. If you've lost sight of your purpose or long-term goals, take some time to reconsider your next steps. It's an ideal day to write a wish list and spend time reconnecting with your dreams.

Wednesday 14th

You may be celebrating a good friend's achievement or news today. Even though you'll feel happy for them, this could throw you into inner turmoil, especially if you're unsure of your value or worth. One of the best things you can do for yourself this summer is to work on your self-esteem.

Thursday 15th

There's a lively and social vibe today. It's likely to be great fun if you're hanging out with friends who make you laugh and entertain you. Being on your own may not be best, especially if you're feeling low. Be around people who lift your mood.

Friday 16th

You may decide to let go of a long-term goal or dream this weekend. This is likely to be connected to travel, study or a spiritual path. Be careful that you don't lose faith in the process and be realistic about your plans. Sometimes, the timing is just not right

Saturday 17th

If your mind is extra lively, it might be a good time to switch off for a while. One way of doing this is to calm your mind through relaxation or meditation. Another way is to limit your time online and switch off the news. Have a weekend free from technology.

Sunday 18th

There's a new moon taking place today, and a theme of secrets and privacy in your astrology. You would be wise to keep your ideas under wraps for now and not give everything away. It's not the right time to launch something new. Wait until the solstice in three days' time.

Monday 19th

You might need to dig deep today and be philosophical if your plans have changed or you're not ready to take a big step down a new path. There's no shame in accepting when life takes a wrong turn and knowing you're not up for a big adventure. Your time will come.

Tuesday 20th

Put yourself and your needs first and recognise when you're being true to yourself. It may not be easy to see a friend set off on a journey or begin a new chapter in life. Try to be pleased for them, but recognise your feelings too and what this arouses in you.

Wednesday 21st

It's the start of your birthday month. The Sun enters your star sign and the cosmic spotlight is upon you. This is the time to celebrate and have fun. It's also the ideal time to focus on your goals and ambitions, your image and appearance.

Thursday 22nd

There's a close link between love and money. You may be tempted by a wealthy new partner, or perhaps you and your other half are keen to improve your joint finances. Be honest about your intentions and crack on with your money-making ventures.

Friday 23rd

The people-person side of your nature takes centre stage today. You may be gossiping with the neighbours or helping out at a charity event. Caring for others often comes naturally to you and can offer you deep fulfilment on a personal level.

Saturday 24th

If you don't have any travel plans lined up, make the most of your life close to home. You could be planning a staycation or be keen to get involved in a community activity over the summer. Whatever your current situation, be proactive and make the most of life.

Sunday 25th

Be careful of overthinking or allowing negative thoughts to dominate. Notice when your mind gets carried away and take control. If your thoughts are running too fast, slow things down via meditation, a long walk or a soak in the bath. Enjoy a healthy escape from the everyday.

Monday 26th

This is not the time to make a rash decision that could impact your financial situation. You don't have to join in with a friend's wild plans; keep your purse strings tight and wait for a safer option.

Tuesday 27th

Talk planet Mercury enters Cancer today, and you might be getting to know yourself on a completely different level. Perhaps you sense a shift in your identity, your confidence or your wellbeing. If you have something important to say, now's your turn to speak up.

Wednesday 28th

When key planets are in water signs Cancer, Scorpio and Pisces, you're in your element. Trust your intuition today and follow your heart over your head. Allow yourself time and space to dream and do more of what you love.

Thursday 29th

The first step towards a long-term goal can be the most important. Today's astrology is urging you to do just that. Make a commitment to yourself and your long-term plans. Start as you mean to go on and build up your levels of discipline and commitment.

Friday 30th

You may find the sea calling you this weekend, or feel drawn towards a day out or venturing further afield. Think of your life as a journey. Try something new, consider your beliefs and say yes to any weird or wonderful invitations that come your way.

JULY

· · · · · · · · · · · · · · · · · ·

Saturday 1st

Something remarkable or miraculous could take place today, creating a unique bond between yourself and a good friend. You might be celebrating an achievement or be presenting an award. Alternatively, you could recognise how wonderful someone is in your life. If so, let them know.

Sunday 2nd

Try not to compare yourself to other people today, and be fully aware of your values and worth. Full moon vibes are strong now when emotions are heightened. Step into your power so you can meet other people halfway. It's time for you to shine.

Monday 3rd

Today's full moon is the ideal time to closely examine your one-to-ones. Look at what works, what doesn't, where you want to commit and where you're ready to move on. Don't take anything for granted on the partnership or relationship front. Instead, take your time and be patient.

Tuesday 4th

You may be up against tough competition somewhere in your life, either personally or professionally. Try not to give in to what other people want or need, and be aware of your strengths. If someone's too much for you and acting intensely, let them know.

Wednesday 5th

As the full moon vibes begin to settle, it's a good idea to consider your current situation more objectively. The full moon always pulls on your heartstrings but to make a clear decision you need to involve your head as well as your heart. Recalibrate yourself today.

Thursday 6th

Being around people who insist on showing off about their possessions or lives can be exhausting. If this is all over your social media, remember that people only tend to post good things about themselves. Nobody's life is entirely perfect under the surface.

Friday 7th

If you've been feeling lonely, it's a good day to reach out to other people and ask for help and support. Arrange a last-minute get-together or ask a friend if they've got time to talk. Don't keep yourself to yourself if you know you'd rather connect with other people.

Saturday 8th

Arrange a date with a difference or go somewhere you've never been before. Invite a friend to go with you or be daring and explore a new experience on your own. Say yes to life, as the more engaged you become, the more you strengthen your purpose and sense of meaning.

Sunday 9th

Set some new intentions and allow yourself to dream. Today's astrology is gorgeous for magical thinking and believing that anything is possible. Allow yourself to be inspired and uplifted by life. Step out of your comfort zone to experience something new. Set off on holiday.

Monday 10th

Life could become considerably livelier from today, whether you're back on the commute or dashing around sorting things out. You could certainly be busy and getting organised at home or in the office. All your communications are about to speed up and fast.

Tuesday 11th

Turn to a good friend if a relationship has stalled. You may just need a short break from someone to gather your thoughts. Quick planet Mercury is in your money zone from today, so leap to it if you have key negotiations, meetings or interviews that could boost your financial situation.

Wednesday 12th

If the theme of change has been running through your friendships recently, there may be more to come. You might be fed up with surprises or people acting unpredictably. Alternatively, you could find that your innovative and wacky friends are a breath of fresh air in your life.

Thursday 13th

Try not to take on too much at the moment. Learn to say no and keep firm boundaries in place. If you're aware you're starting to feel exhausted from wearing too many different hats, stop and reassess what's most important. Perhaps you could delegate some things and free up your time.

Friday 14th

If you're feeling tired or low in energy, you may be delighted when a friend pops up unexpectedly and offers their help. You may not feel you have the energy for a social or group event later on. However, if you make the effort, it will be worth it and you'll get your second wind.

Saturday 15th

You might be enjoying a lazy lie-in or be happy to have nothing scheduled in your diary. As a Sun Cancer, you need to take time out now and again to nurture your soul. You could be up late tonight if you're in the right company.

Sunday 16th

If you're back in the driving seat and your batteries are recharged, line up a new adventure today. A group event or a social get-together could be a lot of fun and you might make some new friends in the process. Embrace life and be part of something special.

Monday 17th

The new moon is in your star sign today, so it could be a time of deep self-recognition when you understand yourself better and know what you want and need to bring you happiness. It's a good date to put yourself and your needs first.

Tuesday 18th

It can be impossible to start over when you're still holding on tight to the past. If a relationship or partnership is holding you back, move on and do whatever's necessary to release any grief or loss. Set your intentions for the months ahead.

Wednesday 19th

When you first catch sight of the crescent moon this week, make a wish, either aloud or written. This is the most important moon of the year because it's all about you. You could wish for a specific amount of money.

Thursday 20th

If travel, study or a legal issue is under the cosmic spotlight, get real about the obstacles involved. It's all well and good wishing for what you want, but in certain areas of life, it could be helpful to find out what's possible and what's not by gathering more information.

Friday 21st

It's a good idea to remember that you can't agree with everyone all the time, and neither will you always be able to convince other people that you're right. Learn to develop patience today rather than getting upset. It might help you to find your people.

Saturday 22nd

You may be missing someone today who you used to rely on a lot. You might be feeling lonely for a partner if you're single, or perhaps you're grieving. If you're in a sentimental mood, ensure you have good support around you and reach out to your friends.

Sunday 23rd

Venus turns retrograde in your money zone today. You could use the next forty days effectively by changing your financial habits if you need to reign in your spending and start saving, or rethink your earnings. Press the reset button and shift your money mindset.

Monday 24th

This is an ideal time to work on valuing yourself and your skills and talents. Ensure you're getting paid what you're worth at work. Notice your self-confidence and what it's attached to. The deeper you dig regarding your beliefs and habits, the more you can uncover.

Tuesday 25th

It's an excellent day to get your family on board with new ways to save money and share resources. You might have children in your life who want to save the planet, or perhaps you're the one who wants to do more and learn some new recycling tips and tricks.

. . . .

Wednesday 26th

Your natural skills and talents are under the cosmic spotlight. Don't dim your light but find ways to creatively express yourself and the person you truly are. It would be a good day to sign up for a new course, to learn a hobby or practise your craft.

Thursday 27th

You might be keen to get in touch with someone from your past today. Often, when Venus is retrograde, old flames or lovers pop up out of nowhere. If you're the one doing the chasing, one particular search could lead you down a deep rabbit hole.

Friday 28th

There are some days when admin and chores take forever. This could be true for you today, so don't demand too much of yourself or your precious time. Staying late after work is only worth it if you're clear about what you can achieve. Don't miss out on the social scene.

Saturday 29th

You might be tidying the house or getting ready for someone coming to visit you. If you're in a relationship, ensure important jobs are out of the way today and prioritise some quality time for the two of you tomorrow. A small purchase could bring beauty into your home.

Sunday 30th

Sit down with your other half and have a serious conversation about your future. That doesn't mean there's anything wrong between you; rather, it's a great day to get serious about your future goals whether you're planning a honeymoon, holiday or a new adventure.

Monday 31st

It's through your networks and group connections where opportunity lies, so make the most of it today. Arrange to introduce your partner to a new group of friends. If you're looking for love, reach out to your loved ones for introductions or expand your social circle.

AUGUST

· · · · · · · · · · · · · · · · ·

Tuesday 1st

Today's full moon highlights money for you. This would be a promising week to discuss financial matters. Work on your money mindset and notice how easy or hard it is for you to attract abundance into your life.

Wednesday 2nd

You may have to make a tough decision today regarding travel or study. This might mean postponing a holiday or course until a future date. Money and resources could be the reason why you need to be sensible. Do what's right for you in the circumstances.

Thursday 3rd

If someone's not talking to you, your best bet could be to find an intermediary or someone who can act on your behalf. There may still be a lot to discuss regarding a holiday or study course. If your plans have changed, try not to be overly disappointed.

Friday 4th

Keep the lines of communication open and turn to the friend you know who might be able to help you. Mid-September could bring a turning point for both travel and study options. Don't write cheques you can't cash.

Saturday 5th

It may be the weekend, but you have positive career astrology today and tomorrow. This could mean you're working overtime, or perhaps you're fired up and raring to go on a new venture or project. This could be linked to your working life or furthering your vocation.

Sunday 6th

Be proactive when it comes to work and money matters. Get the right people on your side and you can make swift progress. Someone may be prepared to lend you the money you need, but ensure it comes with no strings attached. Ideally, find a way to earn the money yourself.

Monday 7th

You may be blown away by someone's offer of help or generosity. One of your best friends or someone you've known for years could be the answer to your prayers. Being around friends with money will encourage you to earn more as their luxury lifestyle will rub off on you.

Tuesday 8th

If you're fundraising for a special event, the key to your success is to widen your social circle. The more people you reach out to, the more chance you have of meeting your target. The best friends are the ones who are willing to have fun without having to spend a lot.

Wednesday 9th

If finances are unpredictable, try to be philosophical about your current situation. There could be a chance to earn big. Ride the rollercoaster of life and be prepared for anything.

Thursday 10th

Today is positively buzzing with good vibes. Be with your friends, catch up with someone close and do whatever works for you to find inspiration and excitement in life. Good news could bring a special reason to celebrate with loved ones.

Friday 11th

You may be feeling out of sorts today and not be in the mood for work or your usual routine. You could say the wrong thing or find that even the most straightforward task takes you way longer than expected. Chill out this evening.

Saturday 12th

You'll feel less stressed today if you spend time getting organised. If yesterday's weird vibe threw you off course, here's your chance to get back on track. You have such an active mind and full emotional range that it's important to have order in your life to bring calm your way.

Sunday 13th

Help could arrive today in the shape of a gift or act of kindness. Today's stars indicate that what you give, you receive in return. Look out for someone coming into your life as a benefactor or fairy godmother. If this inspires you, reach out to help someone close.

Monday 14th

A tense relationship won't be doing you any favours. It's important to start the week on a firm footing and not be thrown off course before you've even left the house. Focus on yourself before anyone else and remind yourself of your value and worth. Give your confidence a boost.

Tuesday 15th

It's up to you who you help out. If there's someone you give money to on a regular basis, you may need to keep this information secret or private. If that works for you, keep it that way. You may be considering setting up a charity donation to further a child's education.

Wednesday 16th

Today's new moon is a glorious symbol for initiating a money-making project and being proactive where finances are concerned. New moon energy is ideal for starting over and turning a new page. Get things moving quickly, especially if unexpected expenses crop up today.

Thursday 17th

Community projects are well-starred, whether you're benefiting from them or doing your bit to help. There may be something you don't want to reveal or speak about. You have every right to remain silent.

Friday 18th

It's an excellent day for learning, studying and putting your clever brain to good use. Keep your mind agile and sign up for a course or class. You may hear about an exciting venture via a new group of friends. The more you join in with others, the more opportunity comes your way.

Saturday 19th

You might be caught up with events close to home or be busy in your local neighbourhood. It's always good to do your bit to help within society but don't forget the ones you love and the people closest to you. Make sure you spend time with family this weekend.

Sunday 20th

The less you have planned today, the better. It will do you the world of good to hang out at home, so relax and take it easy. Plan a day in the garden or lounge around with your family or loved ones. You don't have to spend a lot to do up your home.

Monday 21st

Aim for a gentle start to the working week. You may be enjoying some time off, getting to know your neighbourhood and winding down. Later on, there could be a relationship issue that requires your attention. Step in if someone close is in crisis and be there for them.

Tuesday 22nd

Try not to become too rigid in your beliefs or principles today. There needs to be some wiggle room in your everyday relationships or you could find they wear you out immensely. If you're feeling disillusioned by what you hear, some retail therapy could hit the spot. Treat yourself.

Wednesday 23rd

There's a double whammy of trickster energy today as communication planet Mercury turns retrograde in your communication zone. Back up important files and deal with important correspondence fast. You may have to retake a test or exam, or immerse yourself in your studies.

Thursday 24th

The Sun's move into Virgo turns your attention towards your home life and your community or neighbourhood. You could decide to have a staycation rather than holidaying abroad. Create time for personal relations and don't rush headlong through life.

Friday 25th

You might find it hard to hold your tongue today. Aim for your words to connect rather than divide, and think twice before you speak up. Sometimes, it's the conversations that take you by surprise that are most fulfilling. Create time to talk and meet up with other people.

Saturday 26th

Pay more attention to what you're doing today as your concentration levels could be slow first thing. Make the most of your connections and the people you come into contact with. Being on your own is not an option later on. It might be time to tackle that tough conversation.

Sunday 27th

Spend more time with the ones you love. Introduce new rules to your household so tasks are shared equally and everyone gets their fair say. You benefit from a home life that's comfortable, secure and harmonious, somewhere you can retreat from any sadness out in the world.

Monday 28th

Take note of which friends let you down and which friends are by your side today. Be around people who think outside of the box. Don't get caught up in a challenging situation or drama; you have your own issues to deal with and it's not fair to carry other people's problems as well.

Tuesday 29th

This isn't the best time for financial dealings, as things could go easily awry today. Sometimes, your generosity is misplaced. Consider carefully whether you're doing someone a favour by bailing them out or whether it stops them from taking responsibility.

Wednesday 30th

This is a full moon week, a time when emotions are heightened and a key point in the month for you. You respond to life emotionally, so allow your intuition and emotions to guide you. Be true to who you are during this full moon phase and be around people who inspire you.

Thursday 31st

Consider the bigger picture during today's full moon, whether you're involved in politics or you're pulled towards foreign connections. The stars suggest that you may be keenly aware of your differences rather than what unites you. If in doubt, keep your opinions to yourself.

SEPTEMBER

· · · · · · · · · · · · · · · · ·

Friday 1st

Life close to home may feel increasingly busy and it's sometimes hard to see the wood for the trees. You might need a change of scene to get a different perspective on what's going on in your life, so consider spending some time away, either over the weekend or on a longer break.

Saturday 2nd

It's a good day for being productive and purposeful. You're wise to forget everyday chores and focus instead on the bigger picture. You might be keen to pursue a new career or explore your true vocation. Leap into action and decide how best you can invest in your life.

Sunday 3rd

You may want to get away from someone, either personally or professionally. It's a good day to consider your options and what's best for you. Later on, spend time with someone older, a person you feel comfortable with and to whom you can turn for wisdom and advice.

Monday 4th

Venus turns direct in your money zone today. It's a good date to line up a key conversation, especially if it's linked to money, values or your self-worth. Notice if you've not been valuing yourself highly or if you're avoiding dealing with something important. Change your attitude.

Tuesday 5th

Jupiter turns retrograde in your friendship and group zone. You may make your own rules or laws when it comes to socialising, or perhaps you find it hard to comply with what's required of you. Life may be calling you to rebel, which isn't comfortable for you.

Wednesday 6th

The kindness of strangers could take you by surprise today. Someone may reach out to you unexpectedly and offer praise or a compliment. Be friendly with other people and initiate conversation. Be open-minded and engaging and you may hear exactly what you need to hear.

Thursday 7th

Your emotions or thoughts could run away with you now. Try not to schedule too much into your diary and build in time for daydreaming. If you're feeling unsettled, be kind to yourself. Hold tight to the saying that tomorrow is another day.

Friday 8th

There's a more balanced feel to your stars today, so your mood is likely to shift overnight. A lucky connection might help to remind you of all that's good in your life. Reach out to other people and practise the art of gratitude. Smile at others and you may receive smiles in return.

Saturday 9th

Do whatever feels right to extend your network and get to know people close to where you live. Siblings and neighbours are part of this planetary picture. There may be good news for someone close to you. Someone could leave and move away, which might be a blessing in itself.

Sunday 10th

If you're struggling with a close relationship, make an extra effort to reach out and meet new people today. This might not help your current relationship, but at least you'll have new people in your life and will be able to recognise that your situation is not unique.

Monday 11th

Team up with family or people you live with and share what you have. You may be able to cut expenses when you work together as a team. Keep your eye on your finances and don't let things slip. There is a possibility that someone could try and take advantage of your kindness.

Tuesday 12th

Be wary of an offer that comes your way unexpectedly. If you're typical of your star sign, you prefer to improve your finances slowly and steadily rather than taking a big risk.

Wednesday 13th

You may be back in touch with someone from your past. Alternatively, you may be getting to know someone close on a deeper level and having some serious discussions. This is about looking ahead, committing to plans and deciding how you can best support one another.

Thursday 14th

If you're seeking inspiration, be around other people and let their ideas and excitement rub off on you. Joining in with other people for a good cause is a great way of utilising your current astrology. If there's someone you haven't heard from in a while, get back in touch today.

Friday 15th

Today's new moon highlights travel, transport and education in your horoscope. Take yourself out of your usual surroundings and go somewhere different. It's a lovely new moon phase for setting intentions and drawing up a plan for the month ahead. Take the initiative and keep busy.

Saturday 16th

Earth sign energy kicks in this weekend, bringing with it a flurry of communication. The more organised you are, the more you can get done. It's an excellent time to connect with others. You might be keen to make new friends, meet people online or catch up with old friends.

Sunday 17th

This isn't a time to go it alone in any area of life. Instead, team up with other people to find the support you need and offer advice to other people in return. If you've been hesitating about helping someone out financially, what happens today could convince you either way.

Monday 18th

As a Sun Cancer, you can be scared of being hurt or rejected and you like to know where you stand. If you're in a new relationship, you may recognise that you want another level of commitment. It's a good day to commit to a hobby or be disciplined about a skill or talent.

Tuesday 19th

Try not to get caught up with the hype today or allow something to unsettle you. Take a step back if you feel disillusioned with a lack of compassion in the world or your connections. Don't give up on your hopes and dreams and revisit them when you have more clarity.

Wednesday 20th

Everything could take longer than you expect today and you might end up having to stay late after work. Be realistic with what you can and can't achieve and don't carry a heavy burden by yourself. It's important that you take good care of your health and wellbeing.

Thursday 21st

You could meet someone now who has a transformative effect upon you. It would be a good day to visit a therapist or sign up for a personal growth or development course. Get to know yourself on a deeper level and ask people in your life for an honest opinion.

Friday 22nd

Do your best to stay focused and complete what you start. This might be easier said than done when distraction comes your way. This evening would be ideal for a regular date with the one you love. It doesn't need to be anything fancy, as habit can be deeply comforting for you.

Saturday 23rd

The Sun's move into Libra highlights your home and family zone. This is a reminder that you are at your best when your home environment is peaceful and harmonious. You favour easy relations with the people you live with, and somewhere you can rest, relax and retreat.

Sunday 24th

Emotions could rise today as a close relationship turns intense. Be wary of power games and steer clear of someone controlling. Try to consider your situation objectively and ask a good friend for their opinion or advice. You're wise to let your head rule your heart.

Monday 25th

It's a good week to write things down, make lists and share ideas. Think about what you want to say and get in touch with other people to help each other out. Find the person who's willing to back you if an argument or issue gets out of hand.

Tuesday 26th

You could be in the middle of an emotional drama or financial crisis. If this is true for you, try to take a step back so you can see the situation clearly. It's not a good date to act impulsively, especially in affairs of the heart. Take your time and don't overreact to a tense situation.

Wednesday 27th

Distance yourself from a challenging issue in your personal life and consider the bigger picture instead. Keep your gaze firmly focused on your future plans, where you're heading and why. It could help to get serious about your next steps. There's a sombre mood to the day.

Thursday 28th

This is potentially a fertile period of learning and insight about what you want from life. You may begin to recognise the things you do that aren't good for you. Think of today as a chance to press the reset button on whatever's not working out personally or professionally.

Friday 29th

This feels like a pivotal full moon to make some big decisions regarding your family, your home and your future path. It's time to firm up your plans and let someone know whether you're in or out. This could relate to your home life, a significant relationship or a career move.

Saturday 30th

It's worth holding on to the realisation that you can't please all of the people all of the time. Inevitably, the choices you make now won't impress everyone, especially someone in your family or at home. Even so, you may still decide to put yourself and your wishes first.

OCTOBER

Sunday 1st

Be around the people who understand you the most today. This is likely to be a best friend or someone in your life who can see the positive side of things. You need a cheerleader, a top fan, someone who's on your side whatever is going on for you.

Monday 2nd

It may be hard for you to distinguish between what's real and what's not. Your fantasy life is currently vivid but ensure you have all the facts to hand rather than believing everything you hear. Expect some exciting news from a friend or a group, club or society you belong to.

Tuesday 3rd

If something you heard yesterday left you feeling confused or disappointed, today you're wise to delve deeper to find out more. Do your research before committing, whether this is about a course, a relationship or an adventure. Make sure you know what you're signing up for.

Wednesday 4th

The Moon is in the most introspective zone in your horoscope. This turns your attention inwards and it may be hard to engage with the outside world. It's a good day to stay at home and do whatever's right for you. Be gentle with yourself and shut off your inner critic.

Thursday 5th

Talk planet Mercury moves into Libra today, suggesting you'll find balance and harmony within your family or at home. You may have your home back after a run of visitors, and could be ready to nest. Do less not more, especially if you've been overly busy recently.

Friday 6th

Your benevolent nature comes to the fore today and you could reach out to help a good friend. Ensure that there's a healthy balance in your friendships and you don't give more than you receive. A party or celebration this evening is likely to be a joyous event.

Saturday 7th

Do more of what you love today and don't let the people closest to you call the shots. If you want more time alone or for your projects, ensure this happens. If someone gets cross with you when you're taking care of yourself, this is a red flag warning that all isn't well between you.

Sunday 8th

There are some tricky times to navigate now, perhaps a breakdown, an angry altercation or feeling at the end of your tether. Don't believe you have to be around other people if they're behaving badly, and don't fan the flames of any upset or domestic issue.

Monday 9th

Take a step back today and let strong or intense emotions settle down. Don't collude, but dig a little deeper to find out what's going on. It's not a good idea to be an open book right now. Keep some of your thoughts and feelings to yourself.

Tuesday 10th

If you're typical of your star sign, getting on with other people is important to you. You like to have people on your team and by your side. If there is any kind of falling out or argument now, it could leave you feeling out of sorts. Don't allow yourself to be bullied.

Wednesday 11th

Notice which relationships – personal or professional – support you and which hold you back. Today's stars could indicate a turning point in a significant partnership. Dig deep if you want to move forward together. This is not the time to shy away from a difficult conversation.

Thursday 12th

Passionate Mars moves into Scorpio today. It's potentially a strong and sexy combination, which is good news for your love life, especially affairs and new romance. Whether you know what you want or you're pursued by someone new, it could feel exciting and dramatic.

Friday 13th

If you're involved in a project, your current astrology suggests that a creative block could go away. Perhaps you discover that what you've been working on over the last few weeks and months finally comes together. You're ready to share your new ideas with the world.

Saturday 14th

The weekend begins with a powerful solar eclipse in your home and family zone. A new moon phase with extra oomph represents a chance to start over and begin again. There could be drama within your family or a chance to sort out an ongoing personal issue.

Sunday 15th

You may have an important role to play, perhaps within your family or with people close to you. Certainly, other people will be looking to you to take charge, especially if you're taking care of someone or you're involved in a major home or property-related matter.

Monday 16th

Wait for the eclipse energy to settle before you make a big decision regarding your home or family. There may be a chance to initiate a powerful new chapter in your life. If this is linked to children, trust your intuition about what to do next.

Tuesday 17th

You're the one who's being called forth to do what's right. Step into your power today and take charge of a sensitive issue or delicate situation. Don't listen to other people as their advice could conflict with your decision-making process. It's your call. Trust your inner wisdom.

Wednesday 18th

It might be challenging if you're at work today or cracking on with household chores, but keeping busy could be a welcome form of escape. Put a love or money issue to one side and enjoy the comfort of routine tasks and habits.

Thursday 19th

Ensure that you're being a good role model for other people in your life. The more you look after yourself and stick to your routine, the easier it will be for your family to follow suit. There may be a sense that intense emotions are beginning to settle down.

Friday 20th

This could turn out to be a pivotal weekend when some big decisions need to be made regarding you and your family. It may not matter which direction you take; what's most important is that you make your mind up one way or another, however tough it feels.

Saturday 21st

You may need to decide whether it's time to end a partnership in your life. This could be a contract or connection – for example, a personal trainer or someone you outsource work to. Do whatever's necessary to ensure that your relationships and partnerships work for you.

Sunday 22nd

An intense conversation might take place this weekend and this is not the time to shy away from it. Get to know someone on a deeper level. Ask the question you know will make the most difference to a close relationship. Be fearless when it comes to love.

Monday 23rd

If you're ready for a dose of passion in your life, it could be on the way as the Sun moves into sexy Scorpio today. You're an emotional water sign, and the more you trust in your intuition and follow your instincts, the more emotionally fulfilled you are.

Tuesday 24th

Arrange to do something special over the next few weeks to make the most of the feel-good vibe in your astrology. Be with the people you love, your children or a lover. Sharing experiences creates lasting memories that will nurture you in the months and years to come.

Wednesday 25th

Take an objective look at recent events. If you're aware that strong emotions are no longer helping, find a way to rise above your feelings and see the bigger picture. Dive deep into a good book – you might discover that the philosophers of the past have the answers.

Thursday 26th

If ever there was a time to book a holiday or new experience, it's now. Allow yourself to dream and resolve to overcome any blocks or obstacles that have been holding you back. Don't let someone else's doubts stop you from living the life you choose.

Friday 27th

If you've been caught up with your personal life or family issues recently, it's even more important to focus on your career, vocation and what's next for you. Take the first small step towards a long-term goal. Line up a new project today.

Saturday 28th

Consider what you're passionate about this weekend and do more of it. You may want to spend time with your children or a partner, or perhaps a hobby you've been neglecting. Whatever it is, if it brings you joy, say yes.

Sunday 29th

You may have experienced a lot of drama within your friendships or social life over the last couple of years. Events now suggest a culmination or turning point. You may be more than ready to close a door on a difficult decision regarding romance or children and resolve to move on.

Monday 30th

What are you furious about? What do you feel passionate about? It's important to address both these questions as this is an ideal time to get on your soapbox, vent your feelings and channel your strong emotions as a force for good. Stand up for what you believe in.

Tuesday 31st

You may be dealing with a private or secretive issue today. This could be regarding a love affair or feelings that you have for someone in your life. Even if you don't feel confident, try saying what you feel and see how it sounds. Take a risk as love and friendship are linked.

NOVEMBER
. . . .

Wednesday 1st
You may be in a wistful, sentimental mood and daydreaming about someone special. If you're involved in a love affair, this is likely to be a romantic and passionate time for you. If there's no one on the scene, you may feel a bit sorry for yourself. If so, indulge in some self-care.

Thursday 2nd
Put your best foot forward and make the most of life. Round up your favourite friends for a get-together after work, or do something you love. This may be something that puts a smile on your face, like a hobby. View the glass of life as half full not half empty.

Friday 3rd
This is a lovely date for living life fully and being passionate. Being in a new relationship can be wonderful, full of romance and feel-good vibes. Yes, you may be a tad overconfident but if you're enjoying yourself, you have every right to show off.

Saturday 4th
You could have a big decision to make this weekend about travel and study. A plan may be put on hold when life intervenes. Be patient if this is the case and don't force the issue. Alternatively, you might be keen to change your plans to accommodate the one you love.

Sunday 5th

If you're holding tight to your money and you don't want to spend what you have, it might be a good idea to look a little closer at the reasons why. If nothing's holding you back financially, consider whether you're being too frugal when you don't necessarily need to be.

Monday 6th

Be loving and giving today as what you give, you receive in return. This is a strong date to talk intimately with a loved one and look at ways of tightening the bond between you. It's a positive time to reconnect with a relative or neighbour. Use active listening to learn more.

Tuesday 7th

It's an ideal week for a heart-to-heart and to sort out any muddles or misunderstandings from the previous few weeks. This could apply to your relationship with a child or grandchild. Channel your creativity into inspirational, meaningful activities, or actively seek a spiritual path.

Wednesday 8th

The planet of relating, Venus, enters Libra today, the sign of balance. This turns the spotlight on your home and family, areas dear to your heart. It might be time to extend the olive branch of peace or heal a rift after last month's eclipse activity.

Thursday 9th

This is a lovely day to explore your emotions, examine your feelings closely and reassess what you want when it comes to your one-to-ones. If you are in a long-term relationship or married, make a commitment to one another or renew your vows. Don't test each other's loyalty.

Friday 10th

Talk planet Mercury enters your work and lifestyle zone today, heralding a few weeks when you may be busier than usual. You might pick up a work contract or temporary work position, which could definitely help if you hear that a job is coming to an end.

Saturday 11th

There's some tricky astrology taking place today and you're wise not to do anything foolhardy. Look before you leap and don't rush into a new romance or relationship. There could be an argument or a falling out with a friend. Keep a close eye on children and lovers.

Sunday 12th

You're back in the swing of things after yesterday's strange vibes, and can throw yourself into life knowing that this is exactly the right thing to do. Say yes to a social occasion or group gathering. Be open and enthusiastic with your children, your lover or someone dear to your heart.

Monday 13th

Today's new moon falls in Scorpio, the most passionate zone of your horoscope. This could be the green light you've been waiting for to leap into a love affair. Alternatively, you might be keen to dive deep into a creative activity and to explore your emotions through your art.

Tuesday 14th

This is the new moon phase, a symbol of new beginnings. That doesn't mean everything will work out, but it does mean that it's a good time to take initiative and make things happen. If you sow some seeds, some of them will grow and flourish.

Wednesday 15th

If you're feeling disillusioned with the day job, talk to your family or a close friend. You might need a pep talk or a reminder about where you're heading and why. If you want to change direction, be honest with yourself. A new opportunity could come your way and soon.

Thursday 16th

Make sure that you have a strong support network around you and people who care about you. This always helps when you're going through a wobbly patch as you have someone to lean on. If you're not in a relationship, ensure you have a wide circle of friends to choose from.

Friday 17th

Today's astrology is a reminder to have a life outside of work and your family. Line up an activity for the weekend that allows you to be passionate or romantic, creative or inspirational. It's a great time to enjoy yourself and embrace fun and good times to the max.

Saturday 18th

A Sun-Mars alignment gives you charisma and power in equal measure today. You may find it hard to hold back your passion. When you know what you want, nothing will stop you from going all out to get it. Your willpower is incredibly strong and could inspire someone close to you.

Sunday 19th

You may be diving into unknown territory this weekend and willing to explore new emotions or experiences. Be bold. When you fully harness your courage, you can be a force to be reckoned with. Go all out to take charge of your life and step in to help others.

Monday 20th

Notice which relationships are a healthy influence in your life and where it's wise to move on. If any connection is leaking toxic energy, today's stars could shine a light on what needs to shift or change. Be self-analytical and consider your behaviour.

Tuesday 21st

If you're worried about a child's behaviour, talk to a good friend and get their advice. It's rarely easy for a parent when a child becomes independent overnight but that doesn't mean you can't still talk and be open with one another. A closed book could be hiding a multitude of sins.

Wednesday 22nd

You might be creating firm foundations in your life. Recognise the people who support you and lean on them when necessary. If one relationship has developed into a power game, it may be best to turn down the heat. Do whatever feels right for you.

Thursday 23rd

The Sun moves from water to fire this week, so it's time to focus less on your emotional life and more on getting things done. If you're bored with your current job or routine, start to look at new opportunities. The more flexible you can be, the better. Take the initiative.

Friday 24th

Action planet Mars enters your work and lifestyle zone today and you may immediately notice a shift in your attitude. It's a great time to tackle your life with a positive mindset. Aim to work to live rather than live to work.

Saturday 25th

Draw up a list of things to do and focus on your work and routine, your health and your lifestyle. Being active will help to stabilise your emotions. Being busy could also stop you from dipping into depression.

Sunday 26th

Make time for your friends today and ensure that life isn't all work and no play. Check that you have a healthy balance between the serious and frivolous sides of life. You may already be feeling those celebratory full moon vibes. If so, enjoy them to the full.

Monday 27th

Today's full moon flags up your work/life balance. Do your best to get the help you require, as teamwork and delegation are the keys to your success. This won't always prove easy in the week ahead and you could learn who's a supportive influence and who's not.

Tuesday 28th

If you don't have strong support around you now, you may find it a challenge to get things done. One task too many could quickly overwhelm you. Reach out to other people and ask for what you need. If you can put off important matters until tomorrow, do so.

Wednesday 29th

The moon is back in your star sign today and it's time to ensure that you have a safe harbour, somewhere to land and anchor yourself. When you stop your mind from running away with you, it's easier to plan and make those key decisions that can help to improve your lifestyle.

Thursday 30th

If you're feeling more settled today, you're likely to make the most of your time and achieve what you want quickly and efficiently. Use technology to speed up the process and create new systems in your life – something which could be especially beneficial at work.

DECEMBER

· · · · · · · · · · · · · · · · · ·

Friday 1st

Your close relationships are going to be under the spotlight
in the month ahead. There is an overly generous side to your
Cancer nature but you're wise not to overdo things in the
festive season. Step into your power and ensure that other
people pull their weight.

Saturday 2nd

If you're typical of your star sign, you like to be organised
and might already be thinking about Christmas presents and
beating the crowds at the shops. If you're keen to crack on
with the planning and get your shopping in advance, this is a
good weekend to do so.

Sunday 3rd

You may have to make last-minute changes to today's plans if
someone in the family requires your support. There could be a
relationship crisis taking place, or perhaps they're struggling
financially. Ensure your self-esteem isn't caught up with
what's happening.

Monday 4th

Love planet Venus is on the move this week and enters
Scorpio. This is your horoscope zone that rules romance,
children and all the good things in life. It would be an
excellent week to join a dating agency, put your heart and soul
into a love affair or follow your passion.

Tuesday 5th

If you're involved in a new relationship, you might be keen to make things serious sooner rather than later. It suits you best to know where you stand emotionally. If you're a parent, there could be news of a proposal or a significant new chapter in a child's relationship.

Wednesday 6th

You could be feeling disillusioned today if you're not happy with where your life is heading. Try not to let your mind run away with you and be aware that you may be feeling more emotional or sentimental than usual. Ideally, channel your emotions into something creative or spiritual.

Thursday 7th

You could make life easier for yourself if you get everyone involved in planning the festivities – at work and at home. When you pull together as a team, there's less stress and more enjoyment in the work you do on a daily basis. Rally the troops.

Friday 8th

If there's something you want to say to a partner or good friend in your life, this isn't the time to procrastinate. Events could shift again in a few days and you may find you've missed your opportunity. Good news for someone close gives you a reason to celebrate.

Saturday 9th

If you've got some parties lined up this weekend, or if you're decorating the house ready for Christmas with the kids and grandkids, you're in tune with your stars. Be around people you love and put passion and energy into your everyday life.

Sunday 10th

Don't undervalue yourself – or let someone else do so – today. Your emotions could be stronger than usual and you won't appreciate it if someone takes you for granted. You may be delighted when you hear news of a friend's romance but be worried that it might change things between you.

Monday 11th

The run-up to the festive season can be a frantic time for many people, but the more organised you are, the better. Focus on your wellbeing this week and lower your stress levels where possible. If you're in a job that brings you little fulfilment, take practical action to improve your situation.

Tuesday 12th

New moon energy is good news for you because your star sign is ruled by the Moon. Today's new moon highlights your work and routine, your lifestyle and health, and it's in these areas of your life where you can get busy and make progress. Apply for a new position or job.

Wednesday 13th

Try to keep daydreaming to a minimum today and use all the tricks at your disposal to be methodical and manage your time well. Talk planet Mercury turns retrograde now. Love could be complicated. You may have to wait and be patient.

Thursday 14th

It's not the best time to make a major decision about love or an important partnership once Mercury is in retreat. This could be a time of deep healing and transformation, or perhaps someone goes quiet on you. Whatever your situation, turn inward for answers.

Friday 15th

There's a theme of absence or loss in your astrology. This could mean that you're missing someone who's absent or no longer in your life. The big events of the year are often a time when you feel more sentimental and remember times past.

Saturday 16th

Make time to reminisce or take a trip down memory lane today. You may want to talk about past loves or remember the people who've been important in your life. Alternatively, you could be active today and skip the emotional deep dive. Make sure you do whatever's right for you.

Sunday 17th

You may feel disillusioned with life. Perhaps, you're in a job that's draining you, or you might be out of work and feeling unfulfilled. If so, don't give in to unhealthy habits. If you have a vast well of emotion within you, seek inspiration from a spiritual source or path.

Monday 18th

Keep reaching out to someone special and remind them how much you care. You may worry that your words are being ignored but kindness does make a huge difference. Someone from your past could come back into your life and put a smile on your face.

Tuesday 19th

If the weather's grey outside and your mood ebbs and flows more than usual, turn to things you know will sustain and nourish you. The arts are all sound ways to escape the mundane. Being caring and compassionate could also help.

Wednesday 20th

You may be keen to have your work finished and fast. If so, the stars are on your side and you could be extra speedy today. Some of you may have your eye on a new status or qualification. Be single-minded in your approach and keep your eye on the prize.

Thursday 21st

Today could bring the unexpected. It's not the best date to arrange something special with the one you love. If anything, you may need to have a serious talk to discuss where your relationship is heading. Keep close tabs on a child or lover, especially if they're behaving erratically.

Friday 22nd

The Sun moves into your relationship zone today and you may be more aware of the ties that bind you. This doesn't only highlight personal relationships but your professional partnerships too. Create time for a meeting or conversation this evening and you'll be glad you did.

Saturday 23rd

Retrograde Mercury returns to your work and health zone today. This could mean that you're called back into work, especially if your job is one of the caring professions. It's a reminder to pay close attention to your health and wellbeing. Don't forget what works well for you.

Sunday 24th

If you've been overly indulgent and social in the run-up to the festive season, you might choose to spend a quiet Christmas Eve at home or with your family. You could embrace the symbolic side of the holidays or devote yourself to the person you love, perhaps a partner or parent.

Monday 25th

There may be a part of you that's happy to take a back seat during the festivities and let other people play a leading role. Try not to get overly stressed in the kitchen as it's not your responsibility whether the day's a success or not. If the kids are happy, you're happy.

Tuesday 26th

If you've worn yourself out with the Christmas festivities, you deserve a lie in. Delegate the household chores if a lot of you are celebrating together. This evening, put your feet up and talk about what you want and your intentions for 2024.

Wednesday 27th

If there was ever a time to make an important decision in your life, it's now. This is because of the powerful full moon in your star sign; it's the ideal time to reorient your compass to a direction that suits you as you move forward into the new year and beyond.

Thursday 28th

It could be an exciting end to 2023. Perhaps you receive a proposal or a special gift. Your stars are helping you create the relationship you want for yourself, one that works for you in the here and now. Try not to get caught up in the cut and thrust of everyday life.

Friday 29th

What gets seeded as the year comes to an end could stir your dreams and get you fired up for new beginnings in 2024. If you recognise that you need more support at work or in your everyday life, put those requests into action. Notice the conversations you have around work and health now.

Saturday 30th

You may have a big discussion about money today, but don't think that you have to make a permanent decision. Give yourself the weekend to think things through. If you want to change your job in 2024, this will impact your finances. Work out what's possible and what's not.

Sunday 31st

You may not usually celebrate New Year's Eve, but this year a group of friends or one friend in particular could win you over with their enthusiasm. Even if you only go to the neighbours, see out the new year alongside other people.

Cancer

....

PEOPLE WHO SHARE
YOUR SIGN

PEOPLE WHO
SHARE YOUR SIGN

. . . .

The nurturing influence of Cancer makes this sign the go-to guardian of the zodiac calendar. Teamed with their pioneering instinct, Cancerians have been, and still are, some of the most powerfully empathetic figures in the world, from Nelson Mandela to Malala Yousafzai. The emotional impression that Crabs make is notable, the words of Nobel Prize-winning writers Pablo Neruda and Ernest Hemingway being just two examples. Discover the Cancerians who share your birthday and see if you can spot the similarities.

22nd June

Donald Faison (1974), Carson Daly (1973), Dan Brown (1964), Erin Brockovich (1960), Cyndi Lauper (1953), Meryl Streep (1949), Elizabeth Warren (1949), Kris Kristofferson (1936)

23rd June

Melissa Rauch (1980), Jason Mraz (1977), Zinedine Zidane (1972), Selma Blair (1972), Frances McDormand (1957), Randy Jackson (1956), Clarence Thomas (1948), Alan Turing (1912), Anna Akhmatova (1889)

24th June

Candice Patton (1988), Lionel Messi (1987), Solange Knowles (1986), Vanessa Ray (1981), Mindy Kaling (1979), Robert Reich (1946), Robert Downey Sr. (1936), Chuck Taylor (1901)

25th June

Lele Pons (1996), Sheridan Smith (1981), Busy Philipps (1979), Linda Cardellini (1975), George Michael (1963), Ricky Gervais (1961), Anthony Bourdain (1956), Carly Simon (1945), George Orwell (1903), Antoni Gaudí (1852)

26th June

Ariana Grande (1993), King Bach (1988), Aubrey Plaza (1984), Jason Schwartzman (1980), Paul Thomas Anderson (1970), Sean Hayes (1970), Mikhail Khodorkovsky (1963), Chris Isaak (1956)

27th June

Lauren Jauregui (1996), Matthew Lewis (1989), Ed Westwick (1987), Sam Claflin (1986), Khloé Kardashian (1984), Tobey Maguire (1975), Vera Wang (1949), Helen Keller (1880)

28th June

Kevin De Bruyne (1991), Markiplier (1989), Tamara Ecclestone (1984), Rob Dyrdek (1974), Elon Musk (1971), John Cusack (1966), Kathy Bates (1948), Mel Brooks (1926)

29th June

Kawhi Leonard (1991), Éver Banega (1988), Nicole Scherzinger (1978), Charlamagne tha God (1978), Marcus Wareing (1970), Melora Hardin (1967), Gary Busey (1944), Antoine de Saint-Exupéry (1900)

30th June

Michael Phelps (1985), Cheryl Tweedy (1983), Katherine Ryan (1983), Lizzy Caplan (1982), James Martin (1972), Phil Anselmo (1968), Vincent D'Onofrio (1959), Lena Horne (1917)

1st July

Léa Seydoux (1985), Liv Tyler (1977), Missy Elliott (1971), Pamela Anderson (1967), Diana, Princess of Wales (1961), Dan Aykroyd (1952), Debbie Harry (1945), Olivia de Havilland (1916)

2nd July

Margot Robbie (1990), Alex Morgan (1989), Lindsay Lohan (1986), Ashley Tisdale (1985), Peter Kay (1973), Jerry Hall (1956), Larry David (1947), Hermann Hesse (1877)

3rd July

Sebastian Vettel (1987), Olivia Munn (1980), Patrick Wilson (1973), Tom Cruise (1962), Faye Resnick (1957), Gloria Allred (1941), Franz Kafka (1883)

4th July

Malia Ann Obama (1998), Post Malone (1995), Mike Sorrentino (1982), Elie Saab (1964), Calvin Coolidge, U.S. President (1872), Giuseppe Garibaldi (1807), Nathaniel Hawthorne (1804)

5th July

Dejan Lovren (1989), Tess Holliday (1985), Megan Rapinoe (1985), Pauly D (1980), Amélie Mauresmo (1979), Susan Wojcicki (1968), Claudia Wells (1966), Edie Falco (1963), Paul Smith (1946)

6th July

Eva Green (1980), Kevin Hart (1979), 50 Cent (1975), Jennifer Saunders (1958), George W. Bush, U.S. President (1946), Sylvester Stallone (1946), Tenzin Gyatso, 14th Dalai Lama (1935), Nancy Reagan (1921), Frida Kahlo (1907), Marc Chagall (1887)

7th July
Ashton Irwin (1994), Ally Brooke (1993), Jack Whitehall (1988), MS Dhoni (1981), Kirsten Vangsness (1972), Jim Gaffigan (1966), Jeremy Kyle (1965), Shelley Duvall (1949), Ringo Starr (1940)

8th July
Jaden Smith (1998), Son Heung-min (1992), Jake McDorman (1986), Sophia Bush (1982), Milo Ventimiglia (1977), Kevin Bacon (1958), Anjelica Huston (1951), John D. Rockefeller (1839)

9th July
Douglas Booth (1992), Amanda Knox (1987), Jack White (1975), Courtney Love (1964), Jordan Belfort (1962), Kelly McGillis (1957), Tom Hanks (1956), Lindsey Graham (1955)

10th July
Isabela Moner (2001), Perrie Edwards (1993), Golshifteh Farahani (1983), Jessica Simpson (1980), Adrian Grenier (1976), Sofía Vergara (1972), Urban Meyer (1964), Marcel Proust (1871)

11th July
Alessia Cara (1996), Caroline Wozniacki (1990), Justin Chambers (1970), Lisa Rinna (1963), Richie Sambora (1959), Sela Ward (1956), Giorgio Armani (1934), Yul Brynner (1920)

12th July

Malala Yousafzai (1997), James Rodríguez (1991), Phoebe Tonkin (1989), Topher Grace (1978), Michelle Rodriguez (1978), Anna Friel (1976), Sundar Pichai (1972), Cheryl Ladd (1951), Richard Simmons (1948), Pablo Neruda (1904)

13th July

Rich the Kid (1992), Leon Bridges (1989), Tulisa (1988), Ken Jeong (1969), Cheech Marin (1946), Ernő Rubik (1944), Harrison Ford (1942), Patrick Stewart (1940), Simone Veil (1927)

14th July

Conor McGregor (1988), Victoria, Crown Princess of Sweden (1977), David Mitchell (1974), Matthew Fox (1966), Jane Lynch (1960), Bebe Buell (1953), Gerald Ford, U.S. President (1913), Gustav Klimt (1862)

15th July

Damian Lillard (1990), Travis Fimmel (1979), Gabriel Iglesias (1976), Diane Kruger (1976), Brian Austin Green (1973), Brigitte Nielsen (1963), Forest Whitaker (1961), Linda Ronstadt (1946)

16th July

Luke Hemmings (1996), Gareth Bale (1989), AnnaLynne McCord (1987), Jayma Mays (1979), Corey Feldman (1971), Will Ferrell (1967), Phoebe Cates (1963), Ginger Rogers (1911), Ida B. Wells (1862)